From Hurt to Whole: Overcoming Complex PTSD from Childhood Trauma

From Hurt to Whole: Overcoming Complex PTSD from Childhood Trauma

Copyright © 2023 by **Monday Farouq**

Table of Content

Foreword

Trauma, especially when experienced in childhood, can have profound and lasting impacts on a person's mental health and overall wellbeing. The emotional wounds of adverse early experiences often ripple forward, affecting survivors throughout their lives. Yet with proper support and guidance, healing and thriving after trauma are absolutely possible.

In this groundbreaking book, Dr. Monday Farouq draws on her decades of experience treating and researching complex post-traumatic stress disorder (CPTSD). With compassion and expertise, he provides readers an accessible understanding of trauma and its neurological, psychological and interpersonal consequences. Even more importantly, Dr Monday lays out a practical, evidence-based roadmap for recovering from CPTSD and reclaiming one's life after childhood adversity.

Complex trauma is particularly damaging given its recurring nature during key developmental stages. As Dr. Farouq explains, it literally alters brain structure and functioning. The good news is the brain also maintains plasticity into adulthood, allowing it to be "rewired" in healing ways. By processing traumatic memories within the safe therapeutic space, survivors can start to make sense of the past, transform their relationship to what happened, and release old coping mechanisms that are no longer serving them.

With each chapter, Dr. Farouq validates the challenges of overcoming complex trauma while empowering readers to believe in their ability to do so. He provides concrete skills and exercises tailored to the needs of CPTSD survivors. These include establishing safety through self-care and support networks, learning to self-regulate emotions, addressing unhelpful relationship patterns, finding meaning and purpose in life beyond the trauma, and fostering resilience over time.

While the journey is rarely linear, this book charts a clear course through the recovery process. With Dr. Farouq's thoughtful guidance, readers can finally break free from trauma's grip and move confidently toward reclaiming their whole selves. It is a long-overdue resource that will help countless survivors take that first step from hurt toward healing. Our deepest wounds do not have to define us. There is light waiting on the other side.

Introduction

Trauma encountered early in life can leave scars that last lifetimes. When adversity, abuse, neglect, or other violations occur during childhood or adolescence, they can derail normal development and have enduring impacts into adulthood. Unaddressed, complex trauma becomes complex post-traumatic stress disorder (CPTSD), characterized by self-destructive behaviors, emotional dysregulation, strained relationships, and a diminished sense of self.

Yet, while trauma alters the mind and body in many ways, its legacy does not have to define a person forever. With the right supports, understanding, and tools, survivors can rewrite their stories. Healing is possible.

The Roots of Complex Trauma

Complex trauma stems from frightening, dangerous, and distressing experiences in childhood and adolescence. These may include:

- Prolonged abuse - physical, sexual, emotional

- Neglect

- Living in a war zone

- Growing up with a mentally ill parent

- Multi-generational poverty and deprivation

What makes complex trauma so damaging is its interpersonal nature and pattern of occurring during pivotal developmental phases. Unlike adult PTSD which may stem from discrete traumatic events, childhood complex trauma means being repeatedly violated within essential caregiving relationships. Survival often requires suppressing natural needs for safety and nurturance.

Without secure bonds, children are unable to form a coherent sense of self. Their worldview becomes organized around danger, unpredictability, and self-blame. Biological systems involved in managing stress and emotions get stuck in overdrive. The very architecture of the developing brain is impacted.

In effect, complex trauma freezes survivors in a state of perpetual fight, flight, or freeze. Hypervigilance becomes the baseline. Trust is elusive. Self-worth is obliterated. But beneath this adaptation lies a resilient human spirit yearning to heal.

Common Impacts of Complex Trauma

The consequences of childhood complex trauma are multifaceted, intertwined, and pervasive. They can include:

Emotional dysregulation: Rage, anxiety, sadness, shame, and despair often arise suddenly and without warning. Survivors struggle to calm intense emotions or tolerate distress. Moods swing rapidly and relationships suffer. Numerous individuals resort to alcohol, drugs, self-injury, or other risky actions in search to find relief.

Distorted sense of self: Complex trauma prevents the emergence of a stable, coherent identity. Survivors feel fractured, unreal, and inherently damaged. Negative core beliefs like "I'm worthless" solidify early on. Ongoing denial, minimization, or disassociation from the trauma reinforces this distorted self-perception.

Interpersonal challenges: With attachment and healthy relating disrupted from a young age, survivors struggle to connect with others safely as adults. They are unable to ask for needs, assert boundaries, or cope with perceived abandonment. Some recoil from intimacy altogether. Others seek it out in reckless ways.

Cognitive and somatic impacts: Concentration, memory, and cognitive processing may be impaired. Headaches, gastrointestinal issues, and body aches are common somatic complaints. Sleep is frequently disrupted by nightmares and insomnia. Survivors often push their bodies to the brink with substance abuse and other dangerous behaviors that exacerbate physical and mental health problems.

Re-victimization: Stuck in survival mode, complex trauma survivors can get caught in re-enactment patterns unconsciously seeking mastery or control over their trauma. They repeatedly become entangled in harmful relationships, situations fraught with risk, or actions that undermine their well-being. Each re-traumatization compounds their challenges.

Clearly, the ripple effects of childhood complex trauma are multifaceted and pervasive. They are the natural consequence of extended exposure to situations where basic safety and nurturing were absent. The betrayal embedded in interpersonal trauma further intensifies its impacts. However, with proper supports, survivors can overcome CPTSD to lead fulfilling lives. Healing is possible.

The Biology and Neuroscience of Trauma

To understand complex trauma and begin healing, it is important to examine what occurs in the body and brain when childhood adversity persists over time. Prolonged activation of stress response systems literally alters neural connectivity and function.

However, the brain also retains plasticity into adulthood. Just as trauma conditioned fear and survival behaviors, new experiences can reshape neural pathways in positive ways. The imprint of trauma does not have to be permanent.

The Fear Response

When facing acute threat as children, we reflexively activate well-established neurobiological responses - our survival reactions. The amygdala triggers the sympathetic nervous system to release stress hormones including cortisol and adrenaline. Blood pressure rises. Breathing quickens. We become hypervigilant and primed for fight, flight, or freeze.

When threats pass quickly, this fear response subsides and nervous system returns to baseline. But with chronic childhood trauma, our survival circuits get stuck in overdrive. Our baseline stress hormone levels remain constantly elevated. The amygdala and other midbrain structures literally become enlarged and more reactive over time.

Disrupted Attachment

Early caregiving relationships provide children needed soothing and co-regulation of emotions. With attuned, responsive attachment figures, infants build neural pathways for managing distress. They develop inner working models of relationships as safe and trusting.

Complex trauma utterly disrupts this attachment process. Abuse and neglect teach children that relationships are dangerous, not soothing. With repeated violations by early caregivers, they adapt by suppressing their needs for safety and comfort. But this comes at great cost to mental health.

Impaired Cognitive Functioning

Chronic stress hormones and trauma responses interfere with key brain regions for cognitive functioning. The hippocampus, prefrontal cortex, and other areas suffer reduced volume and connectivity. Memory formation, concentration, planning, and emotional regulation are consequently impaired.

Neuroplasticity allows the brain to be retrained, but initially trauma survivors struggle with academic, professional, and interpersonal spheres due to these cognitive deficits. Supportive interventions can help rewire their neural functioning.

Body-Based Responses

Complex trauma also leaves its mark quite literally in the body. Repeated activation of the sympathetic nervous system causes chronic inflammation, increased heart rate, digestive issues, body pain, headaches, and fatigue. Survivors often dissociate from their body's needs, further exacerbating these somatic complaints.

Integrative approaches emphasize re-establishing mind-body connection to heal trauma holistically. This includes body-based practices like massage, and mindfulness meditation. As the body comes back online, it facilitates restoring emotional balance.

Risk-Taking and Addictive Behaviors

With impaired self-regulation and judgement, trauma survivors often seek intensity in ways that further endanger them. They may engage in unsafe sex, binge eating, crime, physical bullying, or high-risk sports.

Especially with substance abuse, it provides a means to evade emotional distress and memories. But it also leads to worse impairment in executive functioning. An estimated 50-75% of those in addiction treatment have significant trauma histories. Healing trauma is key to overcoming addiction.

Post-Traumatic Growth

The good news is, while trauma changes us neurobiologically, pathways can be rebuilt through therapeutic interventions and new experiences. The brain remains plastic into adulthood. Just as it adapted to seek safety, it can be conditioned towards emotional regulation, healthy relating, and self-actualization.

By releasing maladaptive programming, trauma survivors give themselves the chance to live fully. They can reclaim their power and potential no matter what happened in childhood. This journey is challenging but incredibly worthwhile.

Therapeutic Approaches for Healing

With compassion, knowledge, courage and support, even severe complex trauma can be overcome. Many proven therapeutic frameworks and tools exist to help survivors make sense of their past, transform unhealthy patterns, and move forward in wholeness.

This book provides an overview of evidence-based approaches shown to facilitate healing:

- **Cognitive behavioral therapy (CBT)** focuses on changing unhelpful thought patterns that drive maladaptive emotions and behaviors. Specific trauma-informed CBT approaches directly target stuck points in processing traumatic memories.

- **Somatic therapy** emphasizes tuning into body-based sensations, impulses, and needs. This mind-body reconnection provides a sense of safety and agency often lacking for trauma survivors.

- **Dialectical behavior therapy (DBT)** builds skills for emotional regulation, distress tolerance, mindfulness, interpersonal effectiveness and self-management. It is particularly effective for those with histories of multiple traumas.

- **Eye movement desensitization and reprocessing (EMDR)** facilitates memory reprocessing through bilateral eye stimulation while focusing on specific traumatic incidents. This allows old memories to integrate in less distressing ways.

- **Sensorimotor psychotherapy** targets automatic, unconscious physical responses to triggers. By bringing these into awareness, survivors regain a sense of control over their trauma reactions.

- **Group therapy** provides solidarity and shared understanding needed to overcome the disconnection complex trauma creates. Witnessing others' recovery inspires hope.

- **Medication** can help relieve symptoms of depression, anxiety, and sleep disruption that often accompany CPTSD. But medication alone is insufficient - therapy to process trauma is essential.

The heart of healing is a safe therapeutic relationship. There a survivor can make sense of their experiences, grieve past violation, and emerge with a cohesive identity and renewed trust in relationships. While the road is long, transformation is within reach.

Overview of the Book

This book provides both a big picture understanding of complex PTSD and concrete strategies to address its many impacts. By interweaving educational overview, illustrative stories, and exercises, it offers a blueprint for recovering from childhood trauma.

We begin by exploring complex trauma in-depth, including common causes, symptoms, and neurobiological effects. With this foundation, readers can make sense of their own behaviors, challenges, and pain. Connection and validation help overcome the disconnection and invalidation at the core of complex trauma.

Next the book lays out a step-by-step recovery process with proven techniques to target each dimension of post-traumatic stress. Practical skills for establishing safety, processing memories, regulating emotions, transforming unhealthy dynamics, and restoring self-worth help readers regain power over their mental health.

The last section focuses on transcending trauma by rebuilding meaning, purpose, resilience, and growth. With support, survivors can move from surviving to thriving. Their wounds become sources of wisdom. Their past fuels their future.

At the end of each chapter, reflections and exercises invite readers to actively engage with the recovery process. There are also appendices listing helpful resources and therapeutic tools. While the road is long, the destination - reclaiming wholeness and possibility after trauma - makes the journey worthwhile.

Final Thoughts

Healing complex developmental trauma requires courage, community, and clinical supports. Yet transformation is within reach. The brain remains plastic, primed to be reshaped in positive ways across the lifespan. As survivors process traumatic memories, release old adaptations, and rebuild self-worth, they step fully into the present unbound by the past.

This book provides a comprehensive roadmap to guide that journey in practical, compassionate ways. Each chapter offers education, insights, stories, and skills grounded in research and clinical expertise. While everyone's path is unique, these shared tools light the way.

Childhood trauma casts long shadows. But it does not have to define a person's entire life journey. You have already survived so much and begun the healing process by picking up this book. There is no right pace or perfect path. With courage and support, step by step, you are moving from hurt toward wholeness. The possibility of thriving awaits.

Chapter 1: Symptoms and Impacts of Complex PTSD

Childhood complex trauma undermines a person's emerging identity, sense of safety, and capacity to regulate emotions. By distorting the very foundations of self, it casts ripple effects throughout adult life. Understanding these common symptoms provides validation and direction for the healing journey.

This chapter explores the multi-faceted impacts of complex post-traumatic stress disorder (CPTSD). By shining light on each dimension, we make space for self-compassion. Lasting change becomes possible when we approach ourselves and our behaviors with openness rather than judgment.

Emotional Dysregulation

Difficulty identifying, expressing, and managing emotions is exceedingly common among those with complex developmental trauma. When caretakers do not help infants and children co-regulate their feelings, they grow up unable to independently self-soothe difficult emotions.

For survivors, emotions feel scary and out of control versus useful signals about needs. They are routinely flooded with fight, flight, or freeze reactions. Anger, fear, shame, and sadness consume them. They lack healthy coping outlets and the ability to de-escalate once triggered.

Some main forms of emotional dysregulation stemming from complex PTSD include:

Hyperarousal and Anxiety

The sympathetic nervous system gets stuck in overdrive for trauma survivors. The baseline state becomes one of threat-sensing and panic. Startle responses are extreme while concentration is crippled by free-floating anxiety. Sleep suffers both from hypervigilance and nightmares recalling past trauma.

Mundane experiences like being called on in a meeting or asked a casual question can spur panic attacks. Danger seems to lurk everywhere. Relaxation feels impossible. Medication and behavioral approaches aim to dampen the hypersensitivity of the amygdala and reconnect survivors to a sense of safety.

Intense Anger and Irritability

When needs go unmet as children, it is natural to feel intense frustration. But without supportive caretakers to help process these feelings adaptively, they fester into volcanic rage later in life. Survivors struggle to contain angry impulses and lash out or self-sabotage.

Provocations that would bother others mildly send survivors into blinding fury. They suffer constant irritability and frequent outbursts. Loved ones often bear the brunt of this uncontrolled anger. Medication, cognitive behavioral approaches, and skills training help de-escalate and express anger appropriately.

Emotional Numbness and Shutting Down

To cope with childhood abuse, survivors disconnected from their feelings and needs entirely as an act of self-preservation. But this comes at the cost of living life in an emotional straightjacket. Joy, intimacy, confidence, and other positive feelings remain elusive.

Work with trained therapists is essential to recultivate emotional attunement. Mindfulness practices also help survivors tune back into their moment-to-moment experience. They learn to identify feelings and sensations in their body as gateways back to vitality.

Reactivity and Intense Sadness

Survivors become easily overwhelmed by minimal perceived slights or disappointments. Their emotional responses seem out of proportion to triggering events due to past traumas left unresolved.

Without the ability to self-soothe, they spiral down quickly into profound sadness and despair.

Building internal resources and more adaptive neural pathways allows survivors to respond resilience rather than react intensely. Over time, improved self-regulation lets them experience sadness in balanced ways and ask for comfort from others.

Debilitating Shame

Toxic early experiences intrinsically create a sense of being fundamentally damaged, unlovable, and worthless. This manifests as crippling shame. It drives survivors to hide themselves, sabotage achievements, or beg for reassurance even if they consciously know otherwise.

Processing core traumatic memories that instilled a feeling of shame is essential. As survivors separate past violations from self-worth, they build an intrinsic sense of value within. Self-compassion practices further help counteract undeserved shame.

Heightened Emotional Empathy

Attuning closely to caretakers' emotions for survival makes complex trauma survivors highly empathic to others' pain. They absorb it as their own. Boundaries around feeling immense distress on behalf of people they cannot save become blurred. This "emotional empathy" burns survivors out.

Protecting their energy is essential through practices like loving detachment. Survivors learn they can compassionately understand others' struggles without drowning in them. Their emotional sensitivity becomes an asset not liability.

Emotional Flashbacks

Also called emotional hijackings, these are intense experiences of sudden, overwhelming emotions like rage, terror, or despair without any current triggering event. Instead, the person is flashing back to the emotional state of past traumas. These are terrifying until identified.

Flashbacks feel like going crazy, but they can be managed by using skills to ground and orient back to the present. Over time, processing traumatic memories defuses their raw intensity so emotional flashbacks become less frequent.

Self-Medicating with Substances

Lacking healthy coping mechanisms, many survivors of complex trauma turn to drugs, alcohol, unsafe sex, thrill sports, and other dopamine-spiking behaviors to self-medicate. They pursue intensity to avoid feeling numb or to escape emotional anguish. This often worsens impulsivity and cognitive impairments.

Integrated treatment addressing both addiction and trauma is vital. Medication, behavioral plans, group support, and acquiring life meaning beyond substances helps survivors break free from self-medication.

Distorted Sense of Self

Without attuned caretakers to mirror back a coherent, valued identity in childhood, complex trauma survivors grow up struggling with a fragmented, negative self-concept. They lack an internal compass providing continuity and direction.

Common ways this disrupted identity manifests include:

Feeling Like an Imposter

Carrying toxic shame, survivors are convinced at their core they are undeserving and defective. No amount of external praise or success alleviates this inner sense of fraudulence. They are just impersonating "real" people and fear being exposed. Perfectionism and workaholism help keep up the facade.

Grieving childhood loss of nurturance and validating current accomplishments helps survivors accept their worth. They learn they are not broken, just wounded and healing. Therapy provides corrective emotional experiences.

Feeling Unreal or Disconnected

Reality seems hazy and unreachable due to dissociating to endure childhood trauma. Survivors often describe perceiving themselves as behind glass or unattached to their body which marches through daily motions. They long to feel present and connected.

Grounding techniques like mindfulness and somatic practices help survivors orient to the here and now. Over time, staying present even amidst distress restores a sense of inhabiting one's body and life.

Lack of Agency and Indecisiveness

Raised with no control over safety and needs, survivors enter adulthood struggling with basic self-direction. Making decisions feels overwhelming. Setting boundaries or expressing preferences provokes anxiety. They defer constantly to others.

Small daily choices help build autonomy. Gradually asserting preferences builds confidence. Creating safety in relationships reduces fear of asserting agency. Therapy explores how helplessness was adaptive in childhood.

Identity Disturbance

Complex trauma prevents forming a coherent sense of self across contexts and developmental stages. Survivors feel fragmented, taking on different personas to fit situations. Even core preferences feel elusive.

Exploring each fragmented self state compassionately allows integration of a whole self. Consistent nurturing relationships, values, and life rhythms also help consolidate identity.

Negative Self-Talk and Toxic Shame

Survivors are their own harshest critics, fueled by internalized messages from abusive caretakers. They constantly monitor mistakes and berate themselves with shame. Being kind to themselves feels impossible.

Cognitive behavioral approaches challenge negative self-talk. Self-compassion practices counteract it. They learn to speak to themselves as they would a dear friend - with understanding not judgment for being human.

Feeling Numb, Empty, or Unreal

To endure violations, survivors psychologically vacate the premises of their inner world. But this protective disconnection from trauma also severs access to the full spectrum of emotions and sensory experiences. Life feels flat and meaningless.

As survivors process past traumas, what was once suppressed feelings starts to return. They awaken from the emotional lifelessness that once protected them like a cocoon.

Imposter Syndrome

Despite outward success, internally survivors live with the constant fear their accomplishments are fraudulent. They believe they fooled people into overestimating their abilities and worry about being exposed. This spurs relentless perfectionism and workaholism.

Grieving how childhood trauma severed their sense of inner value helps survivors accept their worth. They learn accomplishments do not define them. Therapy provides mirroring and corrective emotional experiences to consolidate positive identity.

Interpersonal Challenges

Given relational trauma, survivors unsurprisingly struggle with many aspects of connecting to others. Their early programming equated intimacy with danger, preventing healthy bonding. lastingly impact attachment patterns, friendships, work dynamics, and romantic partnerships.

Some common interpersonal challenges stemming from complex PTSD include:

Trouble Reading Social Cues

Hypervigilance to danger left little emotional bandwidth in childhood to pick up on social nuances. Now survivors misread neutral or positive cues as negative and criticism where none exists. They project rejection and respond defensively. Black and white thinking leaves little room for nuance.

What helps is compassionately accepting this tendency as an adaptation for past survival. With practice, survivors can improve social perception, asking clarifying questions rather than assuming negativity. Therapy provides a safe space to take risks and gain interpersonal skills.

Difficulty Setting Boundaries

Fearful of provoking caretakers' anger as children, survivors fail to set needed boundaries as adults. They default to compliance and sacrifice their well-being to avoid rocking the boat. But this bottled up resentment inevitably erupts in outbursts.

Healing involves honoring needs and gradually finding one's voice in relationships. Saying "no" and setting terms of engagement builds trust in one's agency. Survivors accept they can be both kind and assertive.

Expecting Rejection and Abandonment

Past betrayals generate constant fear of relationships ending. Survivors reject others preemptively or interpret any friction as the end. Meltdowns ensue when a friend doesn't text back immediately or a partner wants an evening out. Soothing this panic helps reduce destructive testing behaviors and clinginess.

Difficulty Tolerating Intimacy

Letting others close provokes terror given childhood violation within intimate bonds. Many survivors avoid relationships altogether. Some cycle rapidly between desperate connection and pushing partners away. Building a secure attachment pattern with attuned therapists and friends lays the groundwork for intimacy.

Negative Relationship Patterns

Unconsciously recreating childhood wounds is common – whether as victim or perpetrator. Survivors get caught in dynamics of control, chaos, rescuer-victim, or abuse until they bring awareness to these patterns. Differentiating past from present allows relating consciously.

Taking Things Personally

Childhood emotional invalidation makes survivors hypersensitive to perceived slights. They readily feel criticized, shamed, and rejected when no harm is intended. Healing involves reality-testing these interpretations to reduce reactivity. Over time, feeling secure internally bolsters resilience.

Letting People Down
Terrified of provoking abandonment, survivors overcommit then underdeliver in friendships and work. Helping them balance giving and self-care makes relationships more equitable. Setting incremental challenges builds tolerance for letting some people down sometimes.

Cognitive and Somatic Impacts

In addition to emotional and interpersonal realms, complex trauma alters survivors' cognitive abilities, relationship to their bodies, and health behaviors with long-term fallout. Core brain regions literally shrink and atrophy. The body remains on constant high alert.

Some common examples include:

Concentration and Memory Problems

Neural connections across key brain regions are impaired. As a result, survivors often struggle with short-term memory, attention span, and multi-tasking. Classrooms and workplaces become sites of frustration and shame. Simple instructions need repetition.

Patience, accommodations, and cognitive retraining help compensate for deficits. Creating structure through reminders, sleep hygiene, and minimizing chaos reduces cognitive load. Therapy builds new pathways. Medication can treat underlying attention deficits.

Disorganized Thinking and Time Blindness

Survivors get lost in details, overwhelmed by branching possibilities, and unable to plan systematically. Future and past blur together due to disordered memory patterns. They lose track of time and deadlines, always seeming late and scattered.

External structure again helps compensate through calendars, task lists, and habit stacking. Non-judgmentally accepting limitations prevents compounding them with self-blame. Trauma therapy builds capacity for systematic linear thinking over time.

Physical Hyperarousal and Sleep Disruption

Stuck in fight-or-flight, the body remains jittery, exhausted, and deprived of restorative sleep. Insomnia, nightmares, muscle tension, headaches, and gastrointestinal distress are common somatic symptoms. Survivors need help getting out of emergency mode.

Mind-body techniques like meditation, massage, and psychotherapy provide calming counter-experiences. A wind-down routine before bedtime and sleep hygiene help re-establish restful sleep and health. Ongoing self-care prevents regression.

Somatization of Emotional Pain

Lacking emotional awareness, survivors manifest psychological distress through physical symptoms. These include chronic pain, gastrointestinal problems, migraines, vulnerability to illness, and mysterious medical conditions. No organic cause can be found.

Bringing psychological issues to light through trauma therapy relieves physiological symptoms. Somatic and body-based practices help survivors tune into the mind-body connection, accepting emotions rather than suppressing them. Massage, meditation, journaling, breathwork and regular check-ins with the body facilitate this process.

Disconnected from the Body

To endure violation, survivors psychologically distance from their bodies which bear the wounds of trauma. But this comes at a cost of ignoring interoceptive signals conveying needs and emotions. They push themselves past exhaustion, hunger, and injury.

Re-inhabiting one's body feels frightening after years of disassociation. Somatic therapy provides containment to make this safe. Mindfulness meditation helps survivors tune into signals from within. They learn to care for the body's needs as intrinsic to overall well-being.

Self-Harm and Reckless Behaviors

Lacking self-worth and healthy coping outlets, survivors attack their body or put it at risk through substance abuse, disordered eating, thrill-seeking, and self-injury. Pain provides distraction from internal anguish. Paradoxically, self-harm provides them with a sense of control.

Alternatives like rubbing ice cubes, snapping elastic bands, or holding pungent spices provide stimulation without damage. Building up distress tolerance and self-esteem removes the urge toward self-harm. Therapy explores its roots in trauma.

Compromised Immune System

Prolonged stress taxes all physiological systems, including immunity. Survivors are prone to frequent colds and infections, get sicker than peers when ill, and have chronic vulnerabilities like asthma. Lifestyle changes reduce inflammation while therapy addresses root causes.

Healing Is Possible

This chapter covers some key impacts of complex PTSD spanning emotional, interpersonal, cognitive, and physical realms. Many seem beyond conscious control, breeding helplessness. However, neuroplasticity allows survivors to build new pathways at any age.

Focused skills training in the context of compassionate therapeutic relationships can unlearn old adaptations that now limit life.

While symptoms are challenging, progress begins when we greet ourselves and our struggles with openness not judgment. There lies the seed of change.

#Reflections:

- What complex PTSD symptoms do you identify with most right now? When did you first notice them arise?

- How have these symptoms adapted you for survival in the past? Reflect with self-compassion.

- What impact do your complex trauma symptoms have on different life domains today? What would you like to see change?

#Exercises:

- Make a timeline of when you first noticed different complex PTSD symptoms emerge. What experiences may have contributed to each one?

- Write a letter to yourself expressing understanding and care for the complex PTSD symptoms you currently struggle with.

- Make a list of the top 5 strategies that help you feel better when symptoms are intensified. Keep it somewhere easily accessible.

You deserve support and compassion. There is a path to healing.

Chapter 2: Causes and Risk Factors for Complex PTSD

To make sense of complex trauma's legacy in your life, it helps to revisit its origins. This chapter explores various causes of complex PTSD and risk factors that make children more vulnerable to adverse outcomes. By shining light on these developmental roots, insight and self-compassion can grow.

Childhood Trauma and Abuse

Chronic maltreatment, abuse, and neglect by caregivers are the most direct causes of complex post-traumatic stress disorder (CPTSD). When those entrusted with a child's safety and nurturance instead become sources of danger and distress, developmental trauma is inevitable. Examples of childhood adversities that can cause complex trauma include:

Physical abuse - the repetitive acts of causing pain, bodily injury, or intimidation by a person responsible for caregiving. This includes excessive corporal punishment going beyond reasonable discipline. Physical abuse may leave visible scars, but the emotional scars run even deeper.

Sexual abuse - any sexual contact or exploitation of a child by an adult or older child. Childhood sexual trauma creates lasting feelings of shame, powerlessness, and betrayal at a time when sense of self is forming.

Emotional abuse - persistent harmful interactions with a caregiver who demeans, threatens, rejects, or ignores the child's needs. This undermines self-worth and adaptive functioning. Emotional abuse by itself can profoundly impair development.

Neglect - failure of caretakers to meet a child's basic physical and emotional needs. Physical neglect may involve lack of adequate nutrition, clothing, hygiene, medical care, or supervision. Emotional neglect is the absence of nurturance, attunement, and affection at key developmental phases.

Witnessing violence - being exposed to violence or abuse between caretakers. Even if not directly abused, witnessing domestic violence harms children and causes trauma through destabilizing the home environment and creating a climate of perpetual fear.

Multi-generational trauma - trauma passed down through families across generations when left unaddressed. Current caregiver behaviors reflect their own adverse childhood experiences. Breaking these cycles requires working through root traumas.

In summary, complex trauma originates developmentally from sustained mistreatment within the attachment relationship. The closer to home the danger, the more intense and pervasive the impacts given children's dependence on caretakers. Without intervention, complex trauma sets the stage for lifelong struggles.

Disrupted Attachment

Healthy attachment results from consistent emotional attunement and prompt response to a child's needs and distress signals. Attuned parenting instills self-worth, secure exploration of the environment, and the ability to co-regulate difficult emotions as they arise.

Complex trauma utterly disrupts this attachment process. When caretakers harm, neglect, or fail to comfort children in distress, a sense of basic safety and trust is shattered. Fear and survival replace openness and growth as unconscious attachment motivations. Letting others close feels too risky.

Research shows attachment patterns established in infancy through caregiver interactions exert a lifelong influence over perception, emotion regulation, relationships, and mental health. Disrupted attachment from complex developmental trauma portends future struggles unless repaired through corrective therapeutic experiences.

Social and Environmental Risk Factors

While adverse childhood experiences lie at the root, certain social and family conditions elevate risk for complex trauma occurring and leading to lasting impairment down the road. Being aware of these vulnerabilities provides perspective without blame.

Some key risk factors include:

- Living in poverty

- Family instability and chaos

- Social or cultural discrimination

- Exposure to violence in the community

- Being placed in foster care

- Having a caregiver with untreated mental illness or substance abuse issues

- Being a child born with differences or disability requiring greater caregiving support

- Family stressors like divorce, incarceration of a parent, or death of a loved one

- Role reversal where children become caretakers for adults

None of these factors directly cause complex trauma. Plenty of children facing situational instability, family mental illness, marginalization, or disadvantage grow up relatively unscathed with the protection of other supports.

However, these environmental variables can compound vulnerability in children dependent on caretakers. They constrain resources for attuned parenting, introduce additional sources of stress and potential trauma, or perpetuate multi-generational cycles. Awareness helps breed compassion.

Temperament and Biological Factors

Innate temperament and biological factors represent additional contributors that may increase lifelong susceptibility to complex trauma for some children over others. Nevertheless, it's important not to exaggerate their impact.

Environmental context and parental responses always play a larger role over inborn traits in determining developmental pathways. Still, being aware of inherent vulnerabilities provides insight. Examples include:

Sensitive temperament - Around 15-20% of infants tend to be more reactive to even mild stimuli, feel discomfort acutely, and take longer to soothe. They place extra demands on caregiver attunement and patience. Struggling parents may unfortunately label them as "difficult."

Premature birth - Being born significantly preterm and spending early months isolated in the NICU deprives infants of key bonding experiences. Developmental lags are common even without overt trauma. Establishing secure attachment requires extra sensitivity.

Physical illness or disability - Children with sensory deficits, physical limitations, or chronic health conditions have higher caregiving needs. If these outstrip family resources, the added stressors increase risk for caretaking gaps or outright neglect.

ADHD - Impulsive and hyperactive temperaments frustrate parents who lack understanding of neurodiversity. Harsh punishments or emotional rejection may be imposed on children already struggling to self-regulate.

Genetic variations - Certain allelic differences, like in genes regulating serotonin, dopamine, and cortisol, are suspected to increase reactivity to stress or trauma. However, lifestyle and parenting remain vastly more influential over outcomes.

While aware of these potential innate risk factors, it is essential to remember all children have universal emotional needs. Complex trauma results from caregiver failures meeting those core needs, not from a child's inherent makeup. Compassion and support deserve to be everyone's birthright.

Stages of Development

Timing matters when it comes to childhood trauma. The brain rapidly develops from "bottom up," with more primitive regions maturing before higher-order areas that govern executive functions. Age of exposure to adversity determines symptoms.

Infancy (0 - 2 years) - Trauma disrupts forming a secure attachment style through caregiver attunement and bonding. Later abilities impacted include emotion regulation, stress tolerance, and interpersonal trust.

Early childhood (3-7 years) - Trauma impedes developing autonomy, competence, and self-esteem. Core identity formation is undermined. Later effects involve self-direction, stress reactions, and shame.

Middle childhood (8-12 years) - Trauma interferes with academic and social functioning as children withdraw from normative activities. Long-term educational and occupational impairments often result.

Adolescence (13-17 years) - Trauma, alongside puberty changes, derails identity consolidation and transition to independence. Sexual development is also impacted leading to risky behaviors.

While trauma at any age causes lasting damage, the earlier exposure occurs, the more pervasive and entrenched the outcomes tend to be. However, the brain also retains plasticity across the lifespan. At any point, recovery remains possible through therapeutic change.

Complex Trauma vs PTSD

Complex PTSD stemming from chronic childhood trauma differs in some key ways from adult post-traumatic stress disorder (PTSD) caused by experiencing a single disaster, accident, or act of violence. Understanding these distinctions is helpful for seeking appropriate treatment.

Main differences include:

- **Cause** - complex trauma originates developmentally from ongoing child maltreatment vs PTSD stemming from one or more discrete shocking events later in life.

- **Attachment** – complex trauma directly undermines attachment security vital for childhood development; PTSD does not.

- **Sense of self** – chronic childhood trauma prevents core self-concept and identity formation which are already established in adulthood.

- **Onset** – complex PTSD symptoms manifest immediately following ongoing childhood trauma vs PTSD onset being delayed after a single adult trauma.

- **Dissociation** – children escaping into dissociative states to survive trauma leads to identity discontinuity, depersonalization, and amnesia for past events. This is rarer with single-incident adult PTSD.

- **Emotion regulation** – inability learning to regulate strong emotions evolves from developmental complex trauma. PTSD may provoke intense emotions but does not impair overall affect management capacities.

Complex PTSD requires staging treatment differently from traditional PTSD, with greater emphasis on building relationship skills, core identity, and managing chronic dysregulation. Models like DESNOS (Disorders of Extreme Stress Not Otherwise Specified) identify these complex trauma distinctions.

No Child Is to Blame

In reviewing potential causes and risk factors for complex developmental trauma, it is absolutely essential to state unconditionally – no child is ever to blame for their own abuse or neglect.

Even if temperament, disabilities, or other cited variables added stressors that compromised overwhelmed caregivers, the adult responsibility to nurture and protect young lives always remains. There are no exceptions or excuses for failing children.

Blame rests solely with abusive or neglectful grownups unwilling or unable to meet a child's emotional and physical needs. By remembering this truth, we cultivate compassion for wounded inner children still needing to hear they were and are worthy of love. Healing from trauma begins with self-acceptance, not shame.

#Reflections

- How do your own childhood experiences relate to causes of complex trauma described in this chapter? What formative events do you associate with the onset of symptoms?

- Without judgment, identify any risk factors or developmental vulnerabilities that may have affected your childhood. How could you have been better supported?

- Take a moment to remember you were never to blame for childhood trauma, no matter the circumstances. Affirm your inherent worth.

#Exercises

- Write a letter of understanding and compassion to your younger self about the origins of your complex trauma. Affirm strengths and capacities that enabled you to survive.

- Draw a timeline of key events and periods in your childhood, both positive and traumatic. Identify developmental stages impacted and the emerging symptoms.

- Make a list of nurturing words and comforting actions your inner child still needs to hear and feel now. Identify at least one caring person in your life today who can provide this.

You always deserved love. In connecting to lost parts of yourself with compassion, healing begins.

Chapter 3: The Neuroscience of Trauma and the Traumatized Brain

Trauma changes the brain. To free ourselves from its lingering grip, we must understand the neurobiological impact of early childhood adversity. This chapter provides an overview of how extended or repetitive trauma literally alters neural architecture and functioning.

The brain is both vulnerable and resilient. While early trauma shapes its developing circuitry, neuroplasticity also allows new learning and growth at any age. By restoring neural integration and regulation capacities, we can rewire maladaptive programming. The brain remains plastic across our lifespan.

Demystifying trauma through a compassionate neuroscientific lens helps remove feelings of defectiveness or craziness. We can finally make sense of our struggles. With this understanding comes power to chart a new course guided by self-knowledge, not unconscious reactions.

Brain Basics

The brain develops sequentially from "bottom up" in utero through early childhood. Basic survival circuits solidify first. More advanced cognitive control centers arise later. Trauma disrupts this orderly progression.

Understanding key brain regions helps contextualize the neurodevelopmental impacts of childhood adversity. These include:

The reptilian brain - the brainstem and cerebellum control cardiovascular, respiratory, and motor functions. These primal areas activate instinctive survival responses to perceived threats.

The limbic system - the amygdala, hippocampus, and hypothalamus regulate emotion, memory, motivation, hunger, body temperature, and homeostasis. Trauma impacts these centers profoundly.

The cortex - the neocortex, especially the prefrontal cortex, handles executive functions like planning, reasoning, judgement, focused attention, and impulse control. It is the final aspect to reach full development.

Neural connections across and between regions allow integrated functioning. Trauma impairs connectivity which recovery aims to restore. The brain is designed to endure challenge - with proper support.

The Fear Response

When facing acute threat as young children, reflexive neurobiological responses activate to ensure survival. With trauma exposure, these fear circuits become stuck in overdrive. Understanding the sequence helps us heal it.

1. **Trigger** - The amygdala screens sensory input for any potential danger, erring on the side of over-detecting threats. Past trauma sensitizes it.

2. **Alarm** - If the amygdala perceives a threat, it initiates the sympathetic nervous system, provoking release of stress hormones including cortisol and adrenaline. Blood pressure rises. Breathing quickens. The body mobilizes.

3. **Fight, flight, or freeze** - The hypothalamus triggers one of these instincts. Environmental cues and past survival patterns determine if we stay and battle a threat, flee to safety, or freeze to avoid further harm.

4. **Recovery** - Once a threat passes, the parasympathetic nervous system dampens arousal so systems can return to baseline homeostasis. Heart rate slows. Digestion resumes.

Trauma disrupts this sequence. The parasympathetic failsafe never activates, leaving us trapped in fight, flight, or freeze. Gentle practices like meditation help trigger it to finally resolve the trauma response.

Dysregulated Fear Circuitry

In children exposed to chronic developmental trauma, fear circuits become programmed to activate too easily and remain continuously engaged. This leads to autonomic dysregulation with behaviors stuck in survival mode.

Some key neural impacts include:

- The amygdala enlarges and becomes hyperreactive to mild stressors, bombarding the system with cortisol. This fuels anxiety, agitation, and aggression.

- The vagus nerve fails to relay safety input to the parasympathetic nervous system. We remain in sympathetic overdrive without off switches.

- Executive functioning of the prefrontal cortex is impaired, limiting cognitive regulation of emotions and impulses.

- Chronic inflammation results, compromising immunity and physical health. Neural connections are also disrupted.

- Neurotransmitters like dopamine, serotonin, and GABA are imbalanced, skewing mood, focus, and reward perception.

- Telomeres - protective caps on DNA strands - shorten due to cellular stress, accelerating biological aging.

Through lifestyle changes and clinical therapies, we can calm amygdala reactivity, stimulate parasympathetic recovery, and restore neural integration. The brain maintains its capacity for plasticity throughout one's lifespan.

Disrupted Attachment Circuits

Early parental bonds are meant to instill soothing neural pathways for regulating fear states. Attuned caregivers act as external amygdala for infants, helping calm distress. Chronic childhood trauma blocks this ability to co-regulate.

Structures especially impacted include:

- **The orbitofrontal cortex** - key for modulating emotions, interpreting social cues, and morality. Impairment become evident through addiction, hostility, and behaviors that are anti-social in nature.

- **The anterior cingulate cortex** - part of the limbic system involved in empathy, emotional awareness, and bonding to others. Its disruption after trauma spurs dissociation.

- **Oxytocin receptors** - Oxytocin release prompts warm bonding feelings during parent-infant interactions. Early trauma blunts oxytocin receptor sensitivity, inhibiting attachment and intimacy.

- **The insula** - this region processes body sensations, integrating them with emotions. Trauma impairs insula development, contributing to disconnect between mind and body.

Attachment disruptions ripple throughout life in struggles with relationships, affect regulation, low self-worth, and physical health. Recovery involves grieving these early wounds, then building earned security.

The Immobilized Nervous System

When unable to fight or flee danger as children, many simply freeze as a final instinctive resort. Playing dead protects against predators and shuts down overwhelming pain.

But physically immobilizing comes at a tremendous psychological cost:

- **Dissociation and numbing** - Detaching from the fully embodied experience of trauma leads to ongoing depersonalization, emotional numbing, and surrender of agency.

- **Collapsed nervous system** - Without discharge through fighting or fleeing, trauma energy becomes trapped in the body, collapsing the nervous system into shutdown and exhaustion.

- **Cognitive distortions** - Disconnecting from the integrating functions of the prefrontal cortex impairs reasoning, comprehension, and ability to articulate trauma's impacts.

- **Somatic symptoms** - Muscles freeze around bound trauma energy, leading to chronic pain, mobility restrictions, gastrointestinal issues, and migraine headaches.

Practices like massage and mindfulness meditation help discharge bound fight, flight, and freeze responses so the dynamic nervous system can come back online.

Memory Disruptions

Trauma interferes with hippocampal functioning, disrupting memory consolidation and recall. When excessive cortisol floods the hippocampus, memories fragment into sensation snippets detached from cohesive narrative processing.

Key effects include:

- **Fragmented sensory memories** - Images, sounds, physical sensations, smells, and tastes related to trauma remain vividly encoded in the amygdala without integration. They activate as flashbacks.

- **Narrative memory loss** - The factual storyline and autobiographical context of trauma becomes disjointed or lost entirely. Survivors are left with intense fragments devoid of meaning.

- **Short-term memory impairments** - Focus and concentration are compromised by high cortisol levels impacting the hippocampus. Remembering basic day-to-day information becomes difficult.

- **Dissociative amnesia** - To cope with intolerable trauma, the mind compartmentalizes memories far from conscious awareness. This creates identity discontinuity and amnesia for significant past events.

Therapeutic approaches like EMDR help re-integrate fragmented memories so they can be processed and assimilated in coherent ways. Making sense of the past restores continuity.

Cognitive Impacts

In addition to memory, complex trauma profoundly alters cognitive capacities dependent on the integrative functions of the prefrontal cortex. These include:

- **Difficulty regulating focus and managing distractions** - Traumatized nervous systems struggle to screen out irrelevant stimuli and sustain attention. Easily overwhelmed, concentration wanders.

- **Impaired verbal articulation and alexithymia** - Putting emotions into words becomes very difficult with underdeveloped language centers. Expressive aphasia results.

- **Diminished executive functioning** - Capacities for planning, prioritizing tasks, time management, and delaying gratification are compromised by trauma limiting prefrontal maturation. Starting and completing projects feels tremendously hard.

- **Reduced working memory** - Holding information in mind while performing complex tasks suffers without integration between frontal and limbic regions. Instructions must be repeated. Steps get confused.

- **Limited cognitive flexibility** - Alternating smoothly between mental sets and reacting to changing demands seem impossible due to trauma rigidity. Thinking remains concrete, black and white.

While termed "cognitive," these deficits are not due to low intelligence. Therapeutic approaches help remediate them by strengthening underlying neural connections disrupted by trauma.

Fight, Flight, or Freeze Responses

Our primal survival responses to acute threat - fighting, fleeing, or freezing - have important adaptive functions in life or death situations. But trauma also commonly triggers them in everyday circumstances leading to chronic problems.

Understanding common manifestations empowers us. We can catch and calm inappropriate activations:

Fight - May erupt as anger, rage, or aggression toward others or self. Displays as yelling, shouting, hitting. Activated microexpressions include nostrils flaring, chin jutting forward, narrowed eyes. Shake it out and discharge the energy by signed permission.

Flight - Shows up as avoiding situations, people, places, memories that feel somehow threatening. Headache or fatigue often follows from collapsed mobilization. Softly encourage staying present; danger now is minimal.

Freeze - Appears as deer in headlights paralysis and numbness. Nearly catatonic. Dissociation may follow. Gently guide awareness back into the body; the immobility has passed.

With repetition, we can retrain trauma conditioned neural pathways to respond skillfully, not reflexively, by recognizing these reactions. Greater choice becomes possible.

Neuroception

Neuroscientist Stephen Porges coined the term "neuroception" to describe how neural circuits distinguish safety from danger and activate different biological programs accordingly. With trauma, neuroception goes awry.

In healing, we aim to strengthen capacity for accurately discerning safety so reactivity can settle. Some key concepts:

- The vagus nerve conveys safety input to the parasympathetic nervous system through varied states of arousal. Trauma impairs it.

- Face to face contact, eye gaze, and vocal prosody - tone conveyances underlying speech - signal safety to others. Trauma conditioned people avoid these.

- Proximity, vocalization, and facial expressions indicate safety in social engagement versus defensive mobilization or immobilization. Trauma skews these cues.

- Irrational, disorderly, or immobilized behavior stems from distortions in the fundamental perception of one's surroundings. Provide gentle guidance to re-establish a sense of present safety. Remind them that there is no need for a fight-or-flight response at this moment.

- We can gradually learn to override trauma conditioned neuroceptive misfiring and orient to trustworthy people. New nurturing experiences restore secure neuroception.

With support, our innate neurobiological capacity for detecting safety can come back online, easing trauma's grip. We return from isolation to loving community.

Neuroplasticity

The brain dynamically develops across the lifespan in response to experiences. This lifelong neuroplasticity means we can retrain neural pathways laid down early in trauma. The past does not permanently define the future if we instill new learning.

Some key principles:

- Neurons that fire together wire together. Repeated new thoughts and behaviors build positive neurocircuitry through myelination and physical changes.

- Neuroplastic change occurs through enriching experiences like learning, exercise, creativity, and connection. We can shape neuronal growth in healing ways.

- Lasting neuroplastic change requires consistent repetition over time through behaviors, practices, and relationships. Infrequent insights are insufficient.

- While some sensitive periods exist developmentally, overall plasticity continues lifelong. The brain constantly adapts structurally in response to experience.

- Just as trauma conditioned automatic fear responses, purposeful re-conditioning can cultivate regulation, reason, and reflection.

- Psychotherapy itself fosters neuroplasticity through new emotional experiences, insights, and modeling. The therapeutic alliance becomes a change agent.

We can rewire what trauma wired. Where attention goes, neural firing flows, and the brain changes.

#Reflections

- How does understanding trauma's impact on the brain affect your self-perception and self-compassion?

- Which neurobiological effects of early adversity resonate most with your current challenges and symptoms?

- What encouragement or insights arise knowing your brain retains lifelong capacity for change through new learning?

#Exercises

- Research how secure attachment experiences rewire neural pathways. Identify potential sources of corrective bonding for you today.

- Make a list of daily practices that could build the new circuitry you aspire to: meditation, art, affirmations, etc. Schedule time to engage.

- Notice everyday moments when you shift from fear-based neural firing to peace or empowerment. Write them down.

You can rewire what trauma wired. Your brain remains plastic at any age. Where attention goes, neural firing flows, and the brain changes.

Chapter 4: Establishing Safety, Stability and Self-Care

The journey of recovering from complex PTSD must begin by establishing a sense of physical and emotional safety. Without secure foundations, other therapeutic work remains ineffective, like building on quicksand.

Creating stability through self-care, support systems, financial security, and a soothing daily lifestyle lays the groundwork for deeper healing. Safety lowers survival reactivity so higher reasoning can come back online. A sense of reliable nurturance must develop before we can truly take in care from others.

This chapter explores essential steps for stabilizing foundations early in complex trauma recovery through self-care, basic needs, healthy routines, and absolutely vital psychological and relational protections.

Self-Care Basics

Childhood adversity forces young psyches into a constant state of stress mobilization and chaos. Self-care becomes an alien concept when mere survival preoccupies existence. Reintroducing that loving concept, and making it a tangible practice, proves deeply stabilizing.

Gently begin cultivating basic self-care through:

Nutrition - Regular balanced meals and adequate hydration replenish depleted reserves. Caffeine, sugar, and substances tend to backfire long-term by spiking then crashing the system. Support healthy digestion.

Sleep - Prioritize establishing consistent sleep routines, wind-down time before bed, and keeping the bedroom dark, cool, and screen-free. Address any sleep disorders. Bad sleep perpetuates brain dysregulation.

Movement - Daily walks, stretching, dance, or other gentle movement are tremendously grounding. Aerobic exercise and strength training also benefit the brain. Find activities that feel nourishing.

Nature - Connecting with nature by spending time outdoors in the presence of plants, sunlight, animals, and natural environments has a profound effect on rebalancing the nervous system. Incorporate this into your daily routine.".

Hygiene - Regular bathing, dental care, grooming, and wearing clean clothes bolster self-worth and soothe the senses. Combat trauma's legacy of self-neglect.

Routine - Establishing consistent rhythms around sleeping, eating, activity, and hygiene anchors a feeling of safety and control. Know the week's schedule. Use clocks, planners, alarms to reinforce.

Media - Limit stimulating violent images and content. Avoid graphic news or shows before bed. Monitor use of screens and social media for positive impact, not endless scrolling.

Fulfilling basic needs may seem simple but proves powerfully stabilizing over time. Doing so with compassion allows self-care to penetrate trauma's legacy of unworthiness. You deserve nourishment.

Creating Psychological Safety

In addition to physical replenishment, establishing a sense of psychological safety provides critical secure footing for recovery. Emotional security must be constructed both internally and relationally.

Some key steps include:

Therapy - The therapeutic relationship functions as a secure base, offering consistent empathy, insight, and boundaries. Quality treatment contains intense emotions that arise as past trauma is revisited.

Crisis planning - Having competent crisis support in place, through hotlines, a therapist, 911, or emergency hospital, reduces anxiety around breaking down. Fears of being abandoned when urgently overwhelmed can subside.

Medication - For some, psychiatric medicine provides needed stabilization early in recovery by addressing underlying mental health issues that may accompany complex trauma. This enhances other therapeutic work.

Containment - Learning skills to institutionally contain overwhelming flashbacks, panic attacks, rage, and dissociation prevents these from derailing life. Trauma first aid helps weather storms.

Self-soothing - Identifying healthy self-soothing activities to counter negative arousal is vital. These may include guided imagery, EFT tapping, hugging oneself, breathing exercises. Have some ready before distress escalates.

Support group - Support groups such as 12-step programs, peer support networks, religious congregations, or other recovery groups offer continuous assistance during difficult times. Being able to connect with individuals who understand your experience can be incredibly comforting.

Safety ultimately arises from within. But scaffolding it relationally fortifies a stable sanctuary to do the needed work. Professional guidance navigates this terrain.

Creating Relational Safety

Safety also relies on nurturing connections that foster trust, respect, vulnerability, and unconditional support - the opposite of traumatic bonds. Take time assessing current relationships.

Assess for safety- Are certain relationships unsafe territory where there is manipulation, minimization, or continued control? Establish clear boundaries or remove yourself.

Note red flags - Reactivity, possessiveness, aggression, and extreme hot-and-cold dynamics signal volatility. Proceed with caution. Get professional help leaving if needed.

Communication matters - Seek relationships able to communicate through conflict or discomfort, not withdraw, explode, or make you "crazy." Set the bar higher.

Find secure systems - Connect to reliable communities: spiritual groups, clubs, co-housing, even online forums. These reinforce healthy relating patterns through consistency.

Address enmeshment - Unhealthy merger or triangulation in important relationships is too destabilizing. Strive for boundaries that allow interdependence but maintain selfhood.

Practice saying no - Reclaim choice and rebalance dynamics through refusing unreasonable requests or demands. Just this one word builds autonomy lost in trauma.

Evaluate any relationship causing more harm than healing. You deserve absolute care.

Managing Flashbacks and Triggers

Revisiting past trauma through intrusive flashbacks, body memories, and overwhelming triggers undermines establishing safety in the present. Containing this post-traumatic vortex is essential.

Strategies for reducing retraumatization include:

Identify triggers - Name specific sights, sounds, smells, situations, interactions, even internal states that reliably precede destabilizing symptoms. Increase awareness to mitigate impact.

Grounding skills - Having ready tools like feet on floor, smelling strong scent, holding ice, and exercising stops dissociation and panic by reorienting to the here and now.

Containment imagery - Visualize hurtful emotions and memories sealed in a container, on a TV screen, behind glass, far away. This provides psychological distance and control when flooded.

Physical containment - Wrapping up in a blanket, holding stuffed animal, hiding under weighted blanket, transforms a sense of fragmentation into manageable smallness.

Nature immersion - Stuck nervous systems discharge primal survival energy through movement, senses, and open space found in nature. Being among trees, water, and animals restores.

Crisis intervention - In times of crisis, make sure you have access to emergency support, like a suicide hotline, a trustworthy friend, or a hospital if the situation requires it. Remember, even during the most challenging times, you can overcome them.

With support, compassion, and tools, the intensity of post-traumatic reactions can be endured. Each episode mastered builds resilience for facing the next. They will gradually lessen.

Managing Emotional Intensity

In addition to destabilizing flashbacks, trauma breeds intense emotions like explosive anger, desperate sadness, unshakable anxiety. Daily life becomes consumed. Building healthy regulation is essential.

Some key strategies include:

Identify patterns - Name which emotions become excessive and note reliable triggers. Increase awareness of building explosions or downward cycles.

Early intervention - Address emotions early before they escalate out of control. Use preventive cooling tools like exercise, distraction, music, calling a friend. Stop the momentum.

Somatic practices - Progressive muscle relaxation, soothing music, aromatherapy, and massage return us to the wise messages of the body versus trauma reactions.

Containment skills - Guided imagery to seal up or separate from emotions provides needed distance until they recede naturally. Titrating contact prevents going totally unconscious.

Opposite action - Deliberately shifting posture and facial expressions counteracts sticky emotional states. Smiling triggers biochemical release from anger or fear. Fake it until you make it.

Healthy outlets - Arts, sports, dance, writing, humor provide constructive channels for intense emotions. They move through us without harming relationships or our bodies.

Emotions intensified by past trauma can be moderated. We need not be victims of their riptide. With practice, we can self-correct course when stormy seas arise.

Addressing Defense Mechanisms

In managing the demands of recovery, certain ingrained defense mechanisms arise persistently despite conscious intentions. Having compassion for how they served us in the past while gently discouraging their present use is wise.

Some common defenses include:

Dissociation – Detaching from direct experience through zoning out, shutting down, or leaving your body was once a vital escape. But it breeds disconnection from life. Mindfully sense your feet on the floor.

Projection – Seeing unwanted traits in others protects against uncomfortable self-criticism. But it prevents honest self-reflection. Take responsibility for judgments.

Regression – Reverting to childlike thoughts, behaviors or helplessness may summon a false sense of safety. But change requires risking healthy independence. Identify current age and strengths.

Intellectualization – Removing emotions through excessive analysis distances pain but prevents necessary feelings from arising. Make space to experience.

Minimization – Downplaying trauma's impact or current symptoms stems shame, but prevents addressing needed change. Your struggles are real and valid. Speak openly.

Control – Micromanaging everything restores a lost sense of safety, but exacerbates anxiety and erodes freedom. Tolerate unpredictability as part of healing.

Defenses arise for good reason and offered protection. With compassion, we can acknowledge their past value while encouraging letting down rigid walls to live more fully.

Balancing Productivity and Rest

Complex trauma often breeds either obsessive productivity trying to earn love or hopeless collapse from believing empty efforts. Striking a gentle balance between purposeful activity and guiltless rest proves deeply stabilizing.

Alternate effort and ease - Structure healthy rhythms of engaged focus followed by complete renewal. Flow then rest. Work hard, play soft.

Modulate intensity - Scale effort to about 60-70% capacity to avoid exhausting hypervigilance or hypoactive lethargy. Moderation builds resilience.

Practice non-striving - Choose activities for inherent satisfaction not external results, approval, or avoidance of pain. Savor these islands of present moment focus.

Schedule nothing time - Unstructured spaciousness for stillness, spontaneity, and reflection should be sacred. Don't leave blank spaces vacant. Fill them with being.

Accept laziness mindfully - When lethargy arises, curl up around it softly rather than reacting with harsh self-judgement. Get curious about messages underlying fatigue.

Clarify priorities - Identify how you most want to spend limited time and energy. Align activities accordingly. Delegate unnecessary tasks.

You deserve both gentle effort that structurally supports healing and guiltless rest that honours your humanity. Find this integrating balance.

Financial Security In Recovery

Complex trauma often undermines the executive functioning, education, employment history, and self-confidence needed to achieve financial stability in adulthood. Creating security relieves enormous stress.

Some beneficial steps may include:

- Applying for disability income if unable to sustain work initially in recovery

- Seeking subsidized or reduced-fee housing

- Accessing public transportation vouchers if driving proves too stressful

- Utilizing food banks and community meal programs

- Investigating public health insurance options in your state

- Accepting help from family or churches to cover bills temporarily

- Prioritizing basic needs in budgeting: food, shelter, utilities, medication

- Avoiding credit cards or predatory loans that exacerbate long-term instability

- Saving automatically each month if possible, even small amounts

- Celebrating each step towards independence - they build self-efficacy

- Remembering your intrinsic worth is never determined by income. Healing your psyche holds immeasurable value.

With support, perseverance, and privileging self-care, financial uncertainties can lessen over time. Build security slowly but steadily.

Daily Lifestyle Routines

Complex trauma breeds chaos which maintains neural and physiological survival activation. Constructing simple, consistent daily routines provides calming structure while also modeling that positive change happens gradually.

Some grounding routines to try:

- Morning meditation or journaling

- Eating breakfast mindfully

- Brief midday movement or breathing break

- Preparing a nourishing dinner

- Turning off all screens 1-2 hours before bed

- Waking and going to sleep at the same time

- Light exercise like walking several times a week

- Quality time with a pet every evening

- Reading spiritual or recovery literature before bed

- Saturday morning farmers market or grocery shopping

- Sunday meal planning and laundry

Actively nurturing yourself through humble rituals fosters passive stability from enhanced neural integration under the surface. Healing takes root through repetition.

Soothing Sensory Experiences

Because trauma gets trapped somatically, attending to calming sensory input proves deeply regulating for nervous systems stuck in overdrive. Gentle sensory moments counteract ingrained hypervigilance.

Some nourishing ideas:

- Take a hot cup of herbal tea.

- Listening to comforting nature sounds or soft instrumental music

- Sitting near water watching the flow and ripples

- Smelling essential oil scents on wrist or cotton ball

- Carrying a polished stone, seashell, or worry stone in pocket

- Snuggling under a weighted blanket

- Infusing space with salt lamp glow in the evening

- Letting sand flow through fingers

- Hugging a stuffed animal

- Petting or brushing a soft animal

- Burning beeswax candle

Delight and nourish the senses each day. They are portals out of the trauma vortex back into your body and surroundings. Welcome home.

Inner Child Work

Reconnecting to the innocent essence buried under childhood trauma proves deeply healing. Our inner child remains within us, longing for the nurturance missed the first time around. Providing that now integrates splits.

Some ways to embrace inner children:

- Speak gently inward to their hurts, confusions, and needs

- Offer the safety and comforting you deserved

- Picture cradling them lovingly in your lap

- Write them compassionate letters

- Defend them from critical voices

- Bear witness to their suffering

- Cry over violations enacted upon them

- Provide guidance from your adult self

- Place protective hands over their small shoulders

- Affirm their lovability and worth

- Grieve what they were owed

Though aspects of our inner child remain in pain, we can offer salve now through compassion. Their wounds need not define our present. They can finally be safe and whole.

Why Self-Care Heals

In closing, self-care is not self-indulgent but profoundly medicinal for complex trauma. It instills what was chronically lacking: safety, soothing, predictability, and worthiness. Without these foundations, no other interventions can fully take hold.

Make self-care a priority not because you are weak or need fixing, but because you have inherent value and finally deserve care. Be patient with lapses. Healing is nonlinear. Any step forward creates internal change.

You always deserved love. Now at last you can deliver some measure of that compassion to yourself. In receiving your own care, the journey truly begins.

#Reflections

- What self-care elements feel most essential for you in stabilizing early recovery? Which most need strengthening?

- How could establishing consistent daily routines help provide needed structure? Identify 1-2 you will try implementing.

- Where do you feel safest right now - internally, relationally, environmentally? What needs improvement?

#Exercises

- Make lists of triggers, grounding skills, and self-soothing tools. Keep them handy for when destabilized. Revisit and update regularly.

- Write about a time you successfully endured intense emotions or flashbacks. Identify the skills and inner strengths you drew upon then. Reaffirm your capacity to handle adversity.

- Create a detailed self-care plan addressing nutrition, sleep, movement, social support, nature time, and routines. Refer to it daily. Revise as needed.

You deserve a stable foundation from which to heal. By prioritizing basic self-care, you can construct the secure base missed in childhood. Be patient and celebrate small steps forward.

Chapter 5: Processing Traumatic Memories

At the core of healing complex PTSD is making sense of, grieving, and releasing traumatic memories bound in the body and psyche. This occurs through a phased process of revisiting past events within the safely contained therapeutic space.

As we gently bring traumatic memories into awareness, they can be felt, expressed, translated into language, and integrated into cohesive narratives. Their emotional charge diffuses. What could not be processed during childhood trauma can now complete its course.

This allows us to stop endlessly reenacting fragments of the past through post-traumatic symptoms and unconscious recreated circumstances. We reclaim our life's energy. Healing means no longer remaining hostage to what happened long ago.

Trauma and Memory

Trauma disrupts the brain's normal memory processing. When the amygdala signals threat, stress hormones flood the hippocampus where memories are emotionally encoded and cognitively organized.

Key impairments include:

- Facts cannot form cohesive narrative. Key details remain missing.

- Time sequence becomes fragmented. Events lose logical order.

- Verbal centers shut down. Trauma remains wordless and unprocessed.

- Images, sounds, physical sensations, emotions get encoded intensely without context. They activate later as flashbacks.

Normally memories transfer from short term to long term storage with meaning attached through words. Trauma stops this integration. Explicit narrative memory is lost, even as flashes remain implicitly stuck in the nervous system and body.

Approaches like EMDR help "digest" these undigested memories from the past by introducing bilateral stimulation while consciously connecting images to storyline, emotions, and language. What could not be assimilated during trauma now can.

Phases of Memory Processing

Metaphorically, traumatic memories remain frozen in time until we thaw and transform them through focused work in the protected therapeutic setting. This gradual sequence allows digestion without overwhelm.

1. **Establish safety and trust** - Ensure client feels secure and supported exploring painful content. Build resources to manage emotional intensity. Start where client is ready.

2. **Approach memory slowly** - Revisit peripheral aspects of trauma vs. core events initially. Titrate distress in small doses. Pause often to anchor present safety.

3. **Connect images, senses, feelings** - Name associated vivid images, physical sensations, and emotions linked to traumatic events but detached before. Help integrate these fragments into the whole.

4. **Construct coherent narrative** - Fill in missing storyline details that make logical sequential sense. Attach words to wordless sensations. Translate primitive brain reactions into language for executive brain.

5. **Release through expression** - Provide avenues for safely discharging built-up survival energy through trembling, crying, hitting pillow. Move it out of stuck places with permission. Therapy contains.

6. **Make meaning of suffering** - Help derive psychological insights, purpose, and post-traumatic growth from trauma. Reframe as source of strength and compassion. Rectify injustice internally.

7. **Fully live present** - As past estranged energies integrate, clients inhabit the here and now with full focus and passion. Healing allows engaging life, not just surviving.

With slow patience paced to capacity, the most wounded places can be touched, tended, and revived. We reconnect to our body, spirit, and aliveness.

Titrating Trauma Work

Due to the intensity of traumatic memories, processing work must carefully titrate contact in small doses that allow gentle assimilation over time. Think homeopathy. Too much activation without resolution risks retraumatization.

Components of titration include:

- Address peripheral aspects and timeline first, slowly approximating core events

- Alternate processing past memories with anchoring skills to increase tolerance

- Monitor emotional intensity scaling 1-10. Stay in 4-6 window of moderate intensity that stimulates but does not overwhelm nervous system.

- Pause frequently for self-care practices that provide internal and external resourcing and soothing

- Carefully track somatic cues like heart rate elevating or contractions in belly. Slow down if activating too rapidly.

- Allow time between sessions for integration. Daily trauma processing risks destabilization.

- Emphasize empowering client to set pacing parameters so they retain control over exposure.

Proceeding gradually introduces digestible pieces into consciousness. Like softened taffy, traumatic memories can be gently incorporated for full functioning rather than chronically compartmentalized.

Somatic Approaches

Trauma remains trapped in the body, necessitating somatic approaches to treatment that access nonverbal memory through sensation, movement, and touch. Talk therapy alone cannot penetrate where trauma lives beneath words.

Somatic modalities may include:

SE: Somatic Experiencing - Tracking subtle body cues like trembling, heat, numbness. Titrating dysregulated nervous system activation mildly.

EMDR - Processing memories through bilateral eye movements, taps, or sounds that stimulate integrate left-right brain.

Sensorimotor - Building consciousness of habitual trauma-based physical reactions and introducing skills.

Bodywork - Massage, acupuncture, Rolfing release accumulated trauma physically from tissue.

Dance, drama - Nonverbal expression through movement and creativity bypasses constraints of language.

Art, music - Expressive arts access emotions without limits of words. Creation integrates fragments.

Nature - Being present in natural settings engages senses, innate survival instincts, and openness that restore wholeness.

As thinking brain comes back online, we can finally make sense of past suffering. But first we must thaw out frozen body-held trauma reactions through consistent safe embodiment.

Trauma-Informed Therapy

Not all therapy approaches recognize the unique needs of complex trauma survivors. Educating clients empowers them to seek methods empirically shown to facilitate deep healing versus surface behavioral change.

Key markers of trauma-informed therapy include:

- Understands real but now obsolete adaptive origins of symptoms like emotional intensity, isolation, substance abuse.

- Provides consistent safe relationship to relearn healthy attachment patterns through attuned empathy.

- Prioritizes restoring client's sense of power, choice, and control taken through developmental trauma.

- Skillfully contains difficult emotions that arise during memory processing to prevent retraumatization.

- Proceeds gradually titrating exposure to implement skills building and integration periods.

- Addresses trauma somatically since body holds unresolved reactions. Talk alone is insufficient.

- Recognizes recovery is often nonlinear with ups and downs, not a straight path.

- Integrates strengths-based, empowering practices like EMDR, mindfulness, art and play.

- Allows time for grief over childhood innocence lost and anger over violations by those entrusted with care.

- Builds compassionate understanding of survival programming manifesting now as symptoms.

Educate yourself on clinical approaches shown to facilitate complex trauma recovery. You deserve specialized care.

Finding The Right Therapist

Not just any counselor or generic therapy model necessarily has capacity or training to safely guide trauma processing. Educating yourself facilitates finding an appropriate fit.

Important indicators of strong trauma therapy:

- Specialized expertise and certifications in treating complex trauma and dissociation

- Familiar with neurobiology of trauma and evidenced-based modalities like EMDR and sensorimotor psychotherapy

- Willingness to work slowly and titrate pacing according to client's windows of tolerance

- Commitment to establishing safe environment and trust before processing memories

- Strengths-based language emphasizing "adaptations" versus "symptoms"

- Integral use of mindfulness, art, music, movement to access nonverbal and somatic memories

- Holistic understanding of trauma's impacts on all aspects of client experience

- Appreciation for symptoms as creative adjustments showing resilience and courage

Take time finding a therapist well-versed specifically in complex trauma who feels like a good personality fit. This acts as secure foundation from which to process wounds.

The Therapeutic Relationship

More than any one clinical technique, a secure attachment relationship with a caring, attuned therapist powerfully enables transforming traumatic memory imprints through repeated emotional interactions.

Key elements that foster corrective bonding include:

- Safe environment providing literal physical and emotional refuge in which to explore wounds

- Unconditional positive regard offering nonjudgmental validation regardless of content

- Accurate emotional mirroring and attunement reflecting back inner states

- Reliable consistency meeting at same place and time with no sudden disruptions

- Patience moving at client's pace tolerating intense emotions skillfully

- Trustworthiness keeping confidences and maintaining stable professional boundaries

- Compassion for survivor's immense courage and creative adaptations in managing the unmanageable

- Hope and belief in client's innate capacity to heal and eventually thrive after adversity

Just as developmental trauma warped attachment patterns, reparative bonding with compassionate therapists instills earned secure attachment, allowing risk, expression, and change.

Group Therapy Benefits

Shared connection and witnessing among peers provides another vital format for processing traumatic memory. Groups access supportive power beyond individual counseling relationships.

Key advantages include:

- Alleviates feelings of loneliness and shame by revealing others have similar struggles. Trauma thrives in secrecy.

- Provides round-the-clock emotional support from those who "get it" between sessions.

- Models healthy vulnerability, setting boundaries, taking risks among members.

- Allows quicker cycles of self-disclosure and feedback than individual therapy pacing.

- Enhances vicarious resilience through watching others bravely face their pain.

- Fosters post-traumatic growth by promoting each other's insights and progress.

- Encourages speaking unspeakable trauma directly with profound emotional understanding.

- Teaches relational skills like expressing needs, managing conflict through ongoing interactions.

If available and safe, consider trying group therapy as adjunct to other treatment. Shared humanity heals. You need not walk alone.

Somatic Therapy Tools

Integrating mind and body proves essential in complex trauma given its sensory imprint. Somatic therapy introduces practices that discharge trauma physically through sensation and movement.

Some examples:

EMDR – Bilateral eye movement, tapping or auditory tones stimulate left-right brain integration to digest memories.

Brainspotting – Fixating visual gaze prompts insight and releases trauma stuck in nervous system.

Biofeedback – Electronic monitoring raises awareness of unconscious anxiety held in body.

Breathwork – Conscious breathing into restricted areas opens access to bound emotions.

Neurofeedback – Real-time EEG monitors teach self-regulation of brainwave patterns that ease symptoms.

Expressive arts – Music, art, dance, drama allow nonverbal expression and integration.

Acupuncture – Needle placement restores blocked energetic flow aggravated by trauma.

Massage, Rolfing – Pressure releases accumulated stress lodged physically after trauma.

Nature immersion – Outdoor settings engage senses, movement, and calm inherent survivor instincts.

By integrating mind-body in the present, past trauma imprints become digested. We reconnect with our whole self.

EMDR Overview

Eye Movement Desensitization and Reprocessing (EMDR) serves as one powerful somatic technique for processing memories adaptively. Over 100,000 clinicians have been trained in EMDR worldwide.

Key principles:

- Bilateral stimulation of left-right brain hemispheres through eye movement, taps or tones while recalling trauma allows blocked memory, images, and associated emotions to integrate.

- Information processing system becomes "unstuck" and able to complete a normal cycle of recall, expression, insights and recovery.

- The approach originated after it was noted that lateral eye movements during REM sleep reduce emotional distress from memories.

- eight phases prepare clients to process a distressing memory using distress level, negative belief, and body sensations as metrics of progress. Alternate brief recall with sets of bilateral stimulation.

- Memories lose distressing charge and negative beliefs transform once fully processed. New experiences are consolidated into adaptive memory networks.

- EMDR uniquely allows processing without lengthy detailed description of trauma events making it tolerable for many. But clients must have adequate ego strength first.

Over 24 randomized studies confirm EMDR efficacy in treating both single incident trauma and complex PTSD. It facilitates deep integrated healing.

Therapeutic Writing

Writing about traumatic experiences with guidance provides another avenue for digesting memories through nonverbal expression. We give form to formless pain. Studies confirm emotional and physical benefits.

Some considerations when writing therapeutically:

- Identify an intention to hold focus. What truth needs discovering? What self-compassion is deserved?

- Write in short manageable periods followed by self-care. Titrate like in processing work.

- Allow free uninhibited flow without judgments. Grammar, chronology unimportant. Keep pen to page.

- Notice emotions and body sensations arising as you write. Name them. Stay grounded in the present.

- Write as observer noticing your responses, not immersed in stories. Maintain mindful dual awareness.

- Dialogue with different parts of self through writing. Ask young parts questions.

- Visualize protective forces surrounding you as you write in case emotions intensify. You are safe.

- Alternate processing traumatic material with writing gratitudes to restore balance.

- Share writing with safe people. Break secrecy that gives trauma power. Receive compassion.

Gently crafting coherent narratives from incoherent trauma memories restores order and perspective.

Creative Arts Therapies

Expressive arts access nonverbal language needed to release complex trauma held somatically outside words. They foster new integration pathways through engaging the senses.

Some examples include:

Art therapy – Draw or paint images associated with memories. Use clay, collage. Create visual narrative. Intense emotions can be expressed through color, tactile materials.

Dance/movement – Free the body from habitual holding patterns to discharge fight, flight. Shift out of helplessness through consciously directing movement. Release through shaking, stretching.

Drama therapy – Act out painful scenes from various perspectives. Separate past roles from present identity. Rewrite negative scripts. Practice desired responses.

Music therapy – Sing spontaneously from painful places. Play percussion expressing rage safely. Entrain heartbeat to healthy rhythms. Chant affirmations to drumbeat. Listen to soothing melodies.

Poetry therapy – Craft lyrical metaphors conveying inexpressible feelings. Distill insights into pithy verse. Externalize suffering through symbolism.

Nature therapy – Interact with elements like water, wind, earth to discharge energy. Feel emptiness fill through immersion in wilderness. Journal reflections outdoors.

Creativity engages right-brain holistic processing allowing embodied integration of experiences not fully digested at time of trauma. There are no wrong forms of expression when uncorking pain.

parts work

We contain inner multiplicity as a result of complex trauma. Giving voice to these fragmented younger parts through dialogue provides integration. We reconnect to disowned vulnerability.

Some parts work guidelines:

- Identify protective parts that criticize, numb or sabotage. Thank them for intentions, and discuss current needs.

- Help fight, flight, freeze parts update that danger now has passed. Teach them skills to self-soothe and orient to safety.

- Grieve alongside suffering child parts still in pain. Provide needed compassion.

- Set boundaries with abusive parts that internalized criticism or violation. Affirm self-worth.

- Negotiate between polarized parts that battle within. Find acceptance.

- Help parts lean on your adult strengths and resources now available.

- Support exiled emotional parts to be expressed at last. Hold them with love.

- Retrieve split-off memories and qualities. Welcome them home to wholeness.

- Journal, draw, talk from these inner identities.

- Integrate them over time into the fabric of your whole being.

We can feel compassion for all parts, while encouraging adult insight and empowerment. No part is wrong, just stuck and deserving kindness.

Grieving Trauma

Essential in recovering from any loss, grieving is a process of feelings surging in waves as we slowly metabolize tragedy on emotional and physiological levels. Childhood trauma deserves this cleansing.

Some aspects of grief work:

- **Allow all feelings** – sadness, anger, fear, shame – they need expression versus suppression. Riding waves helps release trauma.

- **Hold hope and pain simultaneously** – The paradox that suffering and joy, death and life coexist expands capacity to bear grief.

- **Take time** – There are no short-cuts with grief. Patience gives experience its full course. Support the slow unfolding.

- **Expect a rollercoaster** – Ups and downs are natural. Grief is not linear. Dosing pain brings equilibrium.

- **Support and ritual** – Community, ceremony, creativity structure otherwise formless and isolating grief. We need companions.

- **Care for your vessel** – Attend diligently to basic self-care needs that grief puts aside like eating, sleeping, moving. Stay embodied.

- **Allow numbness** – Moments of reprieve from anguish revive energy to lean into grief again. Cycling is adaptive.

- **Meaning making** – Later in the process, insight arises about life purpose, post-traumatic growth, and renewed priorities.

Grieving fully honors what we lost and the injustice of it. It frees us from the past's grip. We emerge lighter, and more fully alive.

Why Process Memories?

Processing traumatic memories serves several vital healing functions that free survivors from the past's lingering hold. Understanding these inspires commitment to often challenging work.

- Allows split-off memories to integrate into coherent narrative so the brain can file them adaptively.

- Constructs missing storyline details that make sense cognitively and complete survival responses.

- Attaches language, emotions, meaning to wordless images, physical sensations stuck in nervous system.

- Discharges fight, flight, freeze energy mobilized for survival but still present causing symptoms. Returns agitated nervous system to baseline regulation.

- Distills insights about self and world that create confidence and meaning.

- Transforms trauma from fragmented flashbacks into integrated memories that no longer hijack present functioning.

Chapter 6: Transforming Your Relationship to Trauma

Beyond processing particular memories, a key milestone in recovering from complex PTSD involves changing our overall relationship to past traumatic experiences. We arrive at a place of understanding how it shaped us without allowing it to wholly define us.

This chapter explores practices for relating to your trauma history with greater confidence, ownership, and compassion. We make meaning and build empowering narratives. External events need not directly determine inner worth or potential.

While we cannot erase what happened, we can refuse to be passive victims and fully claim ourselves – both the impacts and transcendence of trauma. Our calibrated responses become conscious choices, not unconscious reactions. We stop handing power over.

Self-Awareness

Cognitively and emotionally separating past trauma from present life represents a pivotal milestone. To get here, increasing self-awareness proves vital. We must know our patterns intimately and catch them as they arise.

Some steps for building mindfulness:

- Keep a daily journal to log thoughts, feelings and behaviors and track themes. Writing extends self-knowledge.

- Set phone reminders periodically to stop and check-in with your inner state. Name emotions and sensations.

- Notice body language, microexpressions, and postures that reveal inner states you may disregard. Our body speaks.

-Pay attention to circumstances, interactions, and qualities in others that reliably trigger reactive symptoms. Bring consciousness to these daily.

- Be curious, not critical when investigating your coping strategies and Automatic Negative Thoughts. See how they served a purpose once.

- Meditate to build capacity for nonjudgmental witnessing of urges, pain, stories as passing phenomena.

- Reflect on dreams which speak in the language of symbol and metaphor to reveal unconscious material wanting attention.

In studying ourselves without embarrassment or denial, understanding dawns. We can finally choose conscious responses instead of just blind reactions.

Journaling

Journaling provides a simple yet potent tool for building self-awareness, tracking changes over time, and integrating memories into coherent narratives. The process is cathartic. Studies confirm mental health benefits.

Some journaling suggestions:

- Pick a neutral time like morning when emotions are calm. Write 3 pages freely without self-judgement.

- Dialogue with different parts of self -critic, abandoned child, inner nurturer - on paper to foster clarity and insight.

- Write about the same trauma memory over time. Note new awareness and decreased charge.

- Delve into metaphors, such as asking yourself, 'If this emotion were weather, how would it be described?'

- Journal dreams and recent memories. Connect imagery to feelings and events. Find threads and meaning.

- Write a letter expressing everything you wish caretakers understood about your trauma and its impacts. Do not send it.

- Release pain safely through destroying pages or burning them ceremonially.

- End each entry with gratitude for strengths and resources today, no matter how small. Affirm hope.

Through consistent processing, epiphanies occur. We construct new empowering narratives that redeem the past.

Working with Flashbacks

Flashbacks represent vivid sensory fragments of past trauma erupting in present life when triggered. Understanding their psychological purpose allows defusing them. We learn to gently guide our system back into current safety.

Consider during flashbacks:

- Recognize flashbacks as attempts to master past trauma. Our mind repeats distressing memories obsessively seeking closure. We need to directly address the original event, not just flashbacks of it.

- Flashbacks indicate traumatic memories that require further processing for smooth integration. Make note of their content for future therapeutic work.

- Regain your focus by affirming to yourself, 'I am currently __ years old and in the present moment. What I'm experiencing is a recollection from the past.' Come back to the here and now.

- Notice which environmental or internal cues tend to precede flashbacks. Increase vigilance around these known triggers.

- Visualize putting memories into a container. They can be opened again later in therapy if needed. You control access on your terms.

- Shift focus fully into your senses. Feel your feet on the ground, the texture of clothing against skin, sounds in the environment. Allow sensory input to ground you in the now.

We can master flashbacks by recognizing their conditioned nature. They lose control when met with calm presence.

Working with Triggers

Triggers catalyze flashbacks and painful emotions by unconsciously reminding us of past traumas in the present. By recognizing triggers, we can defuse them and respond thoughtfully.

Helpful strategies include:

- Maintain a detailed list of situational, relational, sensory triggers and update it over time as awareness deepens. Name each one specifically versus globally.

- Notice precursor warning signs like muscle tension, breath shallowing, heart rate increasing that signal you are being triggered. These provide an early intervention point to avert escalation.

- Assert boundaries around known triggers you cannot control, like leaving situations that regularly activate you until readiness increases. Put your needs first.

- Challenge cognitive distortions triggered by ascribing present motivations and assumptions onto people unaware of your history. Speak up to clarify intent.

- Ask for help identifying blind spots around triggers observable to others through their effects on your mood and functioning. What are you unable to see?

- Develop a coping plan for when triggers arise including self-soothing practices, affirmations, distractions, and calling supportive friends. Have tools ready.

- Remind yourself during triggers "This reaction is about my past, not the present." Increase ability to distinguish then from now.

Triggers lose power when brought into the light of conscious awareness. We free ourselves from reacting on auto-pilot. Responses become choices.

Transformative Justice

Complex trauma inherently contains an element of profound injustice given the violation of basic safety and trust carried out by those with power over dependent children. An essential part of recovery involves addressing this moral dimension.

Some ways transformative justice supports healing include:

- The trauma is explicitly acknowledged as unjust, undeserved, and fundamentally wrong versus minimized or denied. Survivors feel seen and morally validated.

- Responsibility rests fully on perpetrators who violated positions of authority and caretaking. Survivor blame or shame has no place in the narrative.

- The social context that enabled the trauma is analyzed and critiqued as the problem versus locating fault in individual deviance. Larger change is demanded.

- Survivors reclaim personal and collective power through activism, advocacy, protest, education, prevention programs, policy change. Agency lost is reclaimed.

- Public testimony provides cathartic expression and a witness collective that affirms survivors' pain and courage. Silence is broken.

- When possible, acts of restitution are made like formal apologies, financial reparations, memorials. The harm is concretely acknowledged.

- Space is created for survivors to grieve injustice and openly share their truths. They are surrounded by compassion not judgement.

- With support, meaning making involves reframing trauma as a source of empowerment, purpose and protection of future victims. A phoenix rises from ashes.

While we cannot change the past, we can revise our relationship to it by naming the injustice and reclaiming our energy toward greater personal and social justice. We turn pain into power.

Post-Traumatic Growth

In the paradoxical dynamic of complex trauma, our deepest wounds ultimately contain the seeds of our greatest gifts, passions, and callings. From properly tended soil, flowers bloom. Post-traumatic growth describes this phenomenon.

Some common areas of post-traumatic growth include:

- **Compassion** – Having faced cruelty and suffering, survivors often dedicate themselves to serving others contending with similar pain. Your wounds make you the perfect caretaker for certain people.

- **Creativity** – The urge to transcend pain through art, writing, dance, music may emerge. Creative expression allows symbolically conquering trauma.

- **Courage** – Facing past demons builds confidence in one's ability to handle future adversity. Survivors often draw on reservoirs of boldness and resilience.

- **Insight** – Living through hardship confers deep wisdom about life priorities, meaning of existence, and understanding human nature that others do not accrue from comfort.

- **Advocacy** – Many dedicate themselves toward social justice, legal protections, awareness, and prevention regarding the trauma they endured and witnessed. Helping others heals self.

- **Spirituality** – Questioning existence, the journey of the soul, and the nature of evil often leads survivors to profound spiritual inquiry and faith seeking understanding.

We can consciously nurture these positive transformations that bloom naturally from properly mourned loss. Our suffering nourishes purpose. From darkness, light is born.

Meaning Making

An essential task in the integration process involves exploring possible meaning, significance, and metaphoric symbolism of your trauma history. This creates order from chaos.

Some frameworks include:

- Look for hidden gifts and strengths forged through surviving adversity like courage, resilience, sensitivity, leadership or creativity.

- Consider the idea of the "wounded healer" whose capacity to deeply help others comes through experiencing their own pain. Your suffering grows your purpose.

- Reflect on how trauma shaped your values, life philosophy, spiritual seeking, and desire to grow. Let it deepen, not define you.

- View symptoms like hypervigilance as developments of extraordinary watchfulness, boundary setting ability, and protection of the vulnerable based on past violations of safety and trust.

- Recast overcoming trauma as an archetypal hero's journey – passing through a dark night of the soul and emerging stronger in claiming your full power.

- Forgive parents or perpetrators by understanding they likely endured generational trauma. Their own unhealed wounds drove their behaviors. Break cycles.

- Trust your trajectory has meaning beyond what your human mind can presently grasp. There is purpose from forces larger than us.

Resist seeing yourself as only a passive victim of circumstance. Recast your story from despair to agency. You can turn wounds into wisdom.

Empowering Mantras

Repeating empowering mantras and affirmations retrains neural pathways conditioned by past shaming messages that breed unworthiness. We install new positive programming.

Some examples:

- I compassionately release the past's hold over me. I am fully present and at peace here and now.

- I choose empowering beliefs that help me thrive. My mind nurtures, not diminishes me.

- My history shaped but does not define me. I follow my inner wisdom.

- I forgive those who caused me harm through their own unhealed pain. I break destructive cycles.

- Though I cannot change the past, I claim power over the present and future.

- I draw strength from having survived adversity. Courage arises in times of fear.

- Behind my trauma responses, I remain a whole, worthwhile, lovable person deserving care.

- Through expressing my truth, I transform suffering into healing. My voice matters.

- When trauma is triggered, I lovingly comfort myself as I deserved to be soothed then. I am safe now.

- In climbing this mountain, I grow my capacity for compassion, insight and resilience.

Pick phrases that resonate and repeat them through difficult moments to stay grounded in your worth and power. Words condition thoughts, thoughts condition neural networks, and neural networks shape reality.

Inner Child Work

Reconnecting with wounded parts of yourself that fragmentarily splintered in the effort to endure trauma represents a powerful integrative healing process. We release past selves from the chains of survival roles that constrained them.

Some ways to approach inner child work:

- Picture yourself as a child when trauma occurred. Notice their behaviors, feelings, confusion, and needs. Accept this part of you with compassion.

- Dialogue with your inner child. Share your adult insights about events to bring new understanding. Tell them now they are absolutely safe and loved.

- Channel nurturance and protection to the child you once were. Comfort their tears. Sit with their loneliness. Thank them for their resilience. Defend them from self-blame about the abuse. Reassure their fundamental goodness.

- Give your inner child experiences missed that allow playing, feeling carefree, being silly, feeling adored. Let them guide you in activities that fulfill unmet needs.

- Grieve what your inner child went through and still carries in pain. Rage at the injustice of violations against innocence. Aim anger safely where it belongs - at abusers, not yourself.

- Help inner child parts realize they survived, and you are healing. The trauma is over, and life now offers joy and meaning. They have a future beyond past wounds.

By re-owning and caring for exiled elements of self, we become whole. Our inner family comes home.

Parts Integration

Complex trauma leads to splintering into dissociated parts that hold discrete memories, emotions, and behaviors corresponding to past survival roles. Integrating parts restores wholeness.

Some effective approaches:

Map the parts - Identify protective, self-critical, vulnerable, and inner nurturer parts. Notice when each arises and its positive intentions even if actions feel harmful.

Encourage communication - Set up internal meetings or dialogues between polarized parts. Help them listen and understand each other's roles. Find common ground.

Establish boundaries - Restrict harmful behaviors from angry, critical, or self-destructive aspects, all the while recognizing their underlying needs. Guide them toward healthier ways of expression and affirm that they deserve care rather than acting out.

Retrieve memories - When parts hold split off memories, gently help them share burdens. Support safe processing.

Update parts - Show childlike parts photos of you now living a rich life. Help them realize they grew up and have many options.

Channel compassion - Constantly surround all parts, even destructive ones, with understanding of their roles in surviving trauma. They coped as they could.

Foster cooperation - Ask each part how it can help you thrive now versus be stuck in trauma-adopted roles. Help them transfer skills to current challenges.

Practice integration - Do meditations where you invite parts to merge into your core self. Breathe in their colors, qualities and gifts.

With time and patience, fragmentation heals. We reconcile divided elements of self and regain wholeness without losing our hard-won adaptations.

Expressive Arts

Creative modalities like art, music, dance, and writing allow expression of traumatic memories and emotions through nonverbal symbols that access right brain processes inaccessible to words. This fosters integration.

Some examples:

Draw or paint trauma memories - Use color to represent emotions, shapes for people/places, textures to convey sensory elements. Free associate.

Sculpt or mold trauma impacts - Literally shape complex feelings in tactile mediums like clay, playdough. Create new empowering forms.

Dance trauma - Use movement to embody stuck energies of anger, fear, fragmentation. Shake it out through feet.

Write a trauma poem - Craft rhythmic stanzas and lyric imagery conveying intense emotions. Use metaphor and symbols.

Sing the pain - Compose songs or improvise melodies vocally releasing suppressed cries. Play drums or instruments expressing rage safely.

Trauma collage - Assemble found words, images, objects resonating with memories. Juxtapose tangible elements that mirror intangible contents.

Role play - Drama can exorcise trauma by acting out different roles. Practice responses that empower. Revise negative scripts. Direct the play.

Creation channels suffering into something beautiful. We give form to the formless which reduces its control over life.

Ritualizing Recovery

Rituals provide symbolic acts affirming consciousness transitions and identity transformation. Designing personal rituals allows honoring your emergence from trauma.

Examples include:

- Creating ceremony to welcome lost inner child parts back into the whole self

- Writing messages of understanding to caregivers then burning them ceremonially

- Gathering with supportive community to share testimony of trauma burdens now released

- Baptism or immersion in water signifying rebirth and washing pain away

- Dance, music or other celebrations confirming embodiment and freedom

- Taking a healing pilgrimage to places that hold special meaning

- Planting a tree to represent new seeds of growth from past pain

- Receptive meditation surrendering control to spiritual unfolding and life's wisdom

- Ritualizing leaving hurtful relationships, belongings, or identities behind

- Rites of passage into new purpose, work, and community after shedding the past

Infuse transformation with ritual, imagination, metaphor and meaning. Sacred ceremonies structure experiences of psychological death and rebirth. Your healing is holy.

The Nonlinear Path

It is vital to embrace that complex trauma recovery is often a nonlinear, cyclical process alternating between positive gains and distressing setbacks. Understanding this prepares us for the ride. Progress undulates.

Helpful perspectives include:

- Expect periods of increase in symptoms or flashbacks as old defenses loosen and vulnerable emotions surface. This is growth trying to emerge. Stay present.

- When painful content arises, try not turning away or clinging desperately. Let the wave flow through you. Fighting your experience intensifies suffering.

- Remember lapses back into unhealthy coping reflect adaptations that served survival. Meet them with compassion, not shame. You are still healing.

- Growth happens just outside comfort zones. Expect periodically leaving equilibrium as you expand capacity. Discomfort signals ascent.

- New insights begin cognitive shifts that take time to integrate into being automatically. Old patterns persist until replaced through repetition of new.

- If you feel yourself unraveling, return to basics like sleep, nutrition, lowering demands. Trying to power through often backfires.

- Trust your inner wisdom about timing and be patient. Integrating trauma takes time. Progress is still occurring even if subtly beneath surface from day to day.

The path demands courage and compassion. You will reach the other side.

Letting Go of Shame

Unresolved trauma breeds pervasive, corrosive shame that convinces survivors they are fundamentally flawed, unlovable, and defective to their core. Healing involves exorcising this lie. We reclaim our self-worth.

Some practices that counteract shame:

Common humanity – Remember countless good people have suffered. Trauma could happen to anyone. You are not alone.

Self-compassion – Speak gently to yourself as you would a loved one. Recognize pain with care, not criticism. You deserve kindness.

Gratitude – Keep a daily list of all you have accomplished, survived, and strengths that got you here. You are still standing. Appreciate yourself.

Defying labels – Your being transcends any category. You are fundamentally worthy, whole, and good. External judgements cannot define your essence.

Releasing childhood rules – The past conditioned a sense of inherent badness in you. But you make the rules now about your value. Write new ones.

Owning past adaptations – Behaviors that brought shame served necessary functions once. Context matters. Have compassion for the hurting inner child.

Mindfulness – Practice observing shame as mere sensations and stories arising and passing. They do not prove truth about you. Just notice without believing thoughts.

Separating behaviors – Appreciate all people are complex mixes of behaviors - some healthy, some not. Your worth remains despite struggles.

Positive risk taking – Build self-trust by gradually facing situations feared, setting boundaries, and acting from core values. Each success strengthens self-confidence.

Therapeutic processing – In safe relationship, directly explore root causes of shame etched in past trauma. Grieve experiences that instilled a feeling of being dirty, worthless, or deficient. Release identification with abuse.

Shame cannot survive compassion. By holding yourself kindly, self-acceptance grows. You deserve to recognize your inherent worth and humanity.

Reflections

- How has your relationship to past trauma evolved through the recovery process so far?

- What key shifts in awareness and perspective have allowed you to separate it from your present identity and worth?

- What metaphors or meanings around your trauma story bring you comfort and direction?

- How has trauma shaped your values, interests, skills, and sources of meaning without solely defining you?

- What practices or therapeutic approaches have been most helpful for transforming your trauma responses?

- What feels needed to keep deepening your healing journey toward thriving?

Exercises

- Draw or write about your trauma like it was a weather pattern – a storm that passed through but did not remain. How is the forecast different now?

- List empowering affirmative statements about your core self, beneath the trauma story, that affirm your strengths, worth, and humanity.

- Draw or write a letter to your inner child parts explaining your adult perspectives on past events and offering them new nurturance.

- Create art, music, or poetry that symbolizes your process of recovering from past trauma. Let it depict transformation.

- Design a personal ritual to honor your emergence into a new phase of recovery. Enact it in some way.

- If it feels safe, share parts of your recovery story with someone supportive. Break secrecy that gives trauma power. Receive grace.

You are the author of your life. While trauma shaped chapters of the past, you now hold the pen to write the future. Healing allows taking back your power one page at a time.

Chapter 7: Managing Emotional Flashbacks and Triggers

Healing complex developmental trauma requires learning to navigate intense emotional reactions and upheavals when past wounds are triggered. Flashbacks and painful emotions flare up at times without conscious choice.

Yet with education, preparation, and compassion, we can weather these storms. We draw on tools to ground ourselves in the present, modulate arousal, and avoid retraumatization. We come to trust our inner capacity to handle turbulence skillfully.

This chapter explores practical strategies for recognizing, embracing, and soothing emotional flashbacks and triggers in order to integrate them as healing opportunities versus sources of chaos. The skills we build free us over time.

Understanding Flashbacks

Emotional flashbacks describe sudden, overwhelming experiences of rage, shame, fear, or despair that feel disconnected from current circumstances. Physically, the body and nervous system react as threatened, though no actual danger exists.

In truth, emotional flashbacks are subconsciously reliving trauma responses from past violations, losses, and attachment wounds. The mind tries unsuccessfully to integrate these fragments through repetition. Without new understanding, flashbacks tend to recur as unattended trauma energy seeking outlets.

Key dynamics at play include:

- The amygdala fear center activates randomly, flooding the body with stress hormones triggering panic, hypervigilance, aggression.

- Frontal lobes shut down, impairing rational thought and impulse control. The survival brain takes over.

- Fragmented sensory memories stored somatically are released without connection to cohesive narrative or context.

- Emotions attached to past events get transferred onto innocuous current triggers. Reactions feel out of proportion.

While intensely disorienting, emotional flashbacks provide opportunities to repair developmental wounds each time they arise by bringing regulation to dysregulated states. With care, we slowly earn security and agency.

Identifying Flashbacks

The first step in working skillfully with emotional flashbacks involves learning to recognize them. Since awareness gets compromised in survival states, this takes patient tuning into subtle body cues. Over time, we can sense a flashback beginning and intervene quicker.

Some hallmarks of an impending emotional flashback include:

- Sudden onset of arousal symptoms like racing heart, tightness in chest, neck, or stomach

- Emotions that spike rapidly or seem out of context with the actual situation

- Hypervigilance or sense of imminent threat without real danger

- Tunnel vision, dizziness, or losing touch with surroundings

- Feeling small, powerless, defeated or profoundly unsafe in the body

- Shame, self-hate, and sense of being worthless arising for little reason

- The inclination to conceal oneself, escape, engage in self-inflicted harm, or harm another person.

- Mental confusion, difficulty speaking, amnesia or blankness

- Uncontrollable crying, raging, freezing, or emotional numbing

If we can catch even the initial body cues of a flashback, skills have much greater chance of re-regulating the nervous system before it becomes unresponsive. With compassionate awareness, we learn our patterns.

Re-Grounding Strategies

Once an emotional flashback has begun, a key priority becomes re-grounding ourselves in the safer present versus unconsciously reliving the traumatic past. Techniques that orient us to resources here and now help calm survival reactions inappropriate to current circumstances.

Some useful grounding practices:

- Look around slowly and name out loud benign objects you see: table, chair, pencil, book. Describe colors and textures in detail.

- Feel your feet firmly on the floor. Wiggle toes and note the solid ground supporting you now.

- Listen for ambient sounds in the environment: birds chirping, clock ticking, distant traffic. Name each one you notice.

- Smell a strong pleasant scent on a cotton ball held to your nose. Describe the aroma out loud.

- Hold something comforting in your hands like a stuffed animal, soft blanket, or cool stone.

- If safe, hug someone you trust firmly yet gently. Feel their calm breathing and return of embrace.

- Picture people you care for sending you warm, encouraging thoughts. Imagine taking them into your heart.

Simple sensory input helps override trauma circuits pulled into the past. We welcome our mind back to the safety of present life by whatever means work fastest in each moment.

Titration Skills

Besides grounding strategies, an important approach for surviving emotional flashbacks involves titration – carefully moderating contact with overwhelming feelings a little bit at a time to restore a sense of control. We disentangle from inner chaos.

Some useful titration skills include:

- Rate intensity of flashback emotions on a 1-10 scale. Help them ease down incrementally like lowering a spice dose.

- Alternate brief periods of mindfully focusing on the feeling and distracting yourself with an enjoyable activity. This creates a gentle wave rather than constant tsunami of emotion.

- Picture emotions as colors swirling in a jar. Imagine gently pouring a small portion out onto a piece of paper to examine. The rest remains contained.

- Name the earliest emotion you can identify from childhood prompting flashback. Assure your inner child this emotion doesn't need suppressing now. You can handle it together with adult wisdom.

- Allow tears, shaking, or other release of survival energy a little at a time following a sense of internal cues for pacing. Fully feel a few moments, then pause to integrate.

- Use Ichazo's envelopes technique: mentally envision placing flooding emotions into imaginary envelopes in your mind's eye. Close envelopes whenever needed for safety.

Through incrementally titrating contact, we build a track record of tolerating intense inner states. This restores confidence in our resilience. We heal in layers.

Distress Tolerance Skills

When emotional flashbacks peak with overwhelming force, our goal shifts temporarily from modulation to pure survival of the onslaught. Distress tolerance skills help withstand and outlast periods we cannot yet control.

Some beneficial options for tolerating intense states include:

- **Helpful imagery** - Picture emotions as waves that ebb and flow or clouds passing in the sky. Chronic pain as a radio volume dial you turn down. This reduces identification with being the suffering.

- **Containing activities** - Wrap tightly in a blanket, hold ice cubes, take a cold shower for sensory input that matches and counteracts rising inner uncertainty.

- **Intense exercise** - Use the energy by sprinting as fast as safely possible for spurts until raging or frantic emotions reduce in intensity as nervous system tires.

- **Safe boundaries** - Close the door to your room, tell others you are unable to talk now, draw inner boundaries mentally around overwhelming emotions.

- **Distraction apps** - Fidget toys, repetitive phone games, finger breathing, piano key tapping apps redirect nervous system arousal and anxiety temporarily.

- **Time perception** - Flashbacks can feel endless. Remind yourself the pain will pass even if exact duration remains uncertain. You don't have to know when to survive it.

We access inner reserves to simply endure if needed in the faith emotions cannot stay peak activated forever. We summon our warrior spirit. This too shall pass.

Self-Soothing Skills

To counteract the violated trust and unsoothed distress at the core of complex developmental trauma, cultivating reliable self-soothing skills provides perhaps the most direct antidote. We give ourselves what we needed.

Some beneficial forms of self-soothing include:

- **Talking gently to yourself** - Provide compassion you needed as a child through using a kind inner tone, telling yourself "this will pass, I'm here for you, you'll get through this".

- **Soft clothing** - Wrap intensely vulnerable parts in a blanket, shawl, soft socks or fabric that feels soothing.

- **Rocking** - Gently rock body in a chair or curled up on floor to console inner child longing for nurturance.

- **Humming** - Make comforting sounds like humming lullabies or chants to soothe emotions when words fail and panic rises.

- **Stuffed animal** - Hugging a stuffed animal to your chest replicates mammalian instinct to hold young close. We access this innate calming circuitry.

- **Cry** - Let tears flow freely rather than suppressing to release accumulated hurt and pain. Sob into a pillow or while in the shower if needed for privacy.

- **Create comfort** - Make a cozy environment through soft lighting, pillows, favorite scents or foods associated with safety. Appeal to your senses.

Start small. Even minor steps to self-nurture internalize that you deserve care, not neglect or cruelty. With practice, caring for yourself steadily grows more automatic.

Somatic Self-Regulation Tools

Complex developmental trauma becomes wired into the nervous system and body where it dysregulates structures like the reptilian brain, the vagus nerve, and the hypothalamic-pituitary axis. Restoring flexible regulation capacity requires somatic retraining.

Some examples of bottom-up practices that calm the body include:

Breathwork - Conscious exhales stimulate the parasympathetic nervous system. Deep belly breathing in particular (diaphragmatic breathing) activates the relaxation response.

Brainstem massages - Rubbing the back of the neck and cranium areas associated with primal brain structures soothes related nervous system.

Cold water - Brief cold water on face, neck, or back of wrists shifts brainwave states out of fight-or-flight dominance.

Nature - Negative ions, phytoncides, microbes, colors, and electromagnetic fields in natural settings rapidly reduce stress physiology.

Acupuncture - Needle placement in parasympathetic activation points balances energy and stimulates calming oxytocin.

Stretching chest - Open constricted chest with mobilizing poses. This counters collapse and reengages social engagement circuitry.

Belly massage - Massaging intestines prompts vagus nerve activity through gut-brain axis communication. Use healing oils.

Eye movements - Bilateral stimulation of left-right visual fields unfreezes nervous system immobilized during trauma.

When the body regains flexible control, the mind follows. We gently train our nervous system back into safety one practice at a time.

Identifying Triggers

Healing complex trauma requires becoming consciously aware of triggers - people, places, situations, sensations, emotions and behaviors linked to past trauma that catalyze intense reactions and flashbacks in the present. Recognizing triggers reduces blind reactivity.

Some ways to start identifying triggers:

- Notice situations or events that reliably stimulate rages, anxiety attacks, dissociation and other extreme responses. Make an ongoing list of these triggers.

- Pay attention to words, tones, smells, time periods, weather, seasons that tend to precede flashbacks or emotional chaos.

- Look for patterns to your relationships with certain personality types that may symbolize past violators and caregivers.

- Reflect on which specific emotions tend to cascade most quickly into trauma responses like shame into self harm or anger into violence.

- Consider the times of day or circumstances when dysfunctional coping behaviors like substance abuse, binging, or compulsive rituals surface most.

- Check in with supportive others who can point out triggers they observe activating you that you may not perceive internally.

The goal is not to eliminate triggers, which is unrealistic, but reduce blind reactivity when they arise. Their power dissipates as we bring them into the light of consciousness.

Working with Triggers

Once key triggers are identified, we can strategically prepare to defuse and disarm them when encountered rather than unleashing post-traumatic reactions. We respond thoughtfully instead of reflexively.

Some skills for working with triggers:

- Name and validate the underlying emotion, bodily sensation, projection, or past association catalyzed. Creating safety for inner experiences, even painful ones, prevents acting out.

- Remind yourself during triggers "This reaction is about my past, not the present." Increase ability to distinguish then from now.

- Learn to identify "warning signs" like clenched fists, shallow breathing, pressure in the head that signal a trigger has engaged. These provide an early intervention point to avert escalation.

- Institute "time out" steps like leaving a heated situation or distracting yourself temporarily from hot emotions until more in control. Don't react in the heat of activation.

- Request exactly what you need from others - quiet time alone, words of reassurance, a hug - to reduce the intensity of being triggered. Ask for support or accommodations.

- Notice how some dysfunctional coping behaviors serve as "anti-triggers" paradoxically calming threat responses despite causing long-term harm. Understand the pull towards substance use, self-harm, binge behaviors as adaptations. Address the roots.

Triggers lose destructive power only when we bring them into the light of conscious relationships. Their ghosts disappear as we attend to unmet needs.

Managing Hyperarousal and Hypoarousal

Trauma leaves nervous systems stuck in extremes of hyperarousal and hypoarousal. Purposefully calming excess stress and excess numbing restores balanced functioning. We expand the window of management between shutdown and overwhelm.

Hyperarousal management:

- Decrease sensory input like bright lights or loud noises that feed agitation.

- Slow cognitive stimulation way down. Limit demands. Simplify choices. Provide clear direction.

- Require calming routines before bedtime. No screens. Soothing music or meditation.

- Offer angled enclosed spaces that feel protective versus triggering more vulnerability. Hide spaces help discharge fight energy.

- Encourage brief bursts of intense movement like stomping feet or ripping paper to discharge mobilized survival energy in harmless ways.

- Teach paced belly breathing as portable way to prompt relaxation response and vagal tone. Practice consistently when relaxed to make default response.

Hypoarousal management:

- Play energizing music and turn lights bright to awaken nervous system.

- Introduce novel, unpredictable experiences that prompt engagement like art, dance, travel. Make lists of small adventurous steps.

- Encourage mindfulness anchoring in the present moment through senses versus drifting dissociatively.

- Rub skin with textured fabrics or take hot/cold showers to stimulate sensations.

- Invite emotional expression through eyes, face, vocal tones, gestures. Help words connect to feelings.

- Require just enough daily life activation to stretch withdrawn comfort zones slightly while preventing avoidance.

Staying patiently present helps nervous systems emerge from frozen or flooded extremes. We hold compassion for the adaptations while encouraging return to flow.

Improving Frustration Tolerance

Given complex trauma often compromises the ability to handle disappointments and daily upsets calmly, building frustration tolerance becomes an essential recovery skill. We strengthen capacity to contain reasonable upset without losing equanimity.

Some suggestions for improving frustration tolerance:

- Observe how minor irritations can rapidly escalate hypervigilance into extreme, catastrophic thinking. Recognize this recurring pattern. Consider this question: "What if I could skillfully address the root cause of my frustration before it reaches a point of becoming an unmanageable situation?"

- Identify physical and emotional signs you are reaching intolerance like muscles tensing or thoughts turning negative. Take this cue to use cooling strategies.

- When feeling distressed, steer clear of self-critical statements like 'what's the matter with me?' as they can intensify your frustration. Instead, respond with self-compassion, saying, 'This is challenging, but I can be understanding and patient.

- Visualize frustration as a wave that naturally builds then crests and subsides. Breathe through the rise and fall without getting submerged in negative storylines. Stay present.

- Share healthy vulnerable expressions like "I feel so frustrated when..." vs. lashing out. Ask for help soothing big feelings versus handling alone.

- After irritations, center back into body with mindful breathing and sensing feet on ground. Regain stability.

- Celebrate small successes tolerating discomfort without regression into trauma responses. Build confidence you can manage upset.

Frustration happens. Expect it, allow it, breathe through it. With care and practice, we expand capacity to contain ordinary daily upsets.

Skillstreaming

Given the multi-faceted nature of complex trauma, building skills in managing emotional flashbacks, identifying triggers, grounding, calming nervous systems, modulating arousal, practicing self-care, and tolerating distress represents an ongoing practice.

Integrating such skills into daily life relies on repetition and lifestyle habits. Some suggestions:

- Maintain a list of helpful practices and coping strategies. Review and revise regularly.

- Schedule daily time to devote for preventative calming practices like self-soothing, mediation, or journaling versus only when in crisis.

- Find a skills development group focused on applying techniques between sessions. Share how strategies are working over time.

- Aim to master one skill well per month. Build sequentially. Download apps that teach portable practices.

- During flashbacks, pick the one or two strategies that could help fastest in that moment. Simple is better when overwhelmed.

- Develop plans for when certain emotions intensify (anger plan, panic plan, suicidal thinking plan) with specific skills. Have ready to implement.

- Reward skill attempts, not just successes. Notice judgments that shame inevitable mistakes in learning. Progress builds gradually.

- Ask supportive others to help identify skill deficits and strengths to target and leverage respectively. Where do you need more practice? What inner resources can you draw on?

Surviving a flashback or trigger even just one time builds neural wiring to help handle future episodes. Over time, regulation becomes second nature.

Self-Compassion

Essential in the ongoing journey of healing complex developmental trauma is relating to ourselves, including lapses and times of regression, with profound compassion rather than harsh self-judgment. Shame retraumatizes.

Some ways to build compassionate inner dialogue:

- Offer encouraging words to yourself as you would a dear friend during their difficulties. We all deserve this kindness.

- Notice self-blame that feeds trauma's legacy and redirects anger onto yourself versus the original causes. You do not deserve added shame.

- Remember symptoms like emotional reactivity represent creative adaptations in context. They reflect striving for wholeness under duress, not personal failures.

- Acknowledge the enormous strength it has taken to survive. You have accomplished so much already through incredible courage and resilience. This remains true even during periods of backsliding.

- Allow space to grieve losses and violated trust that bred survival

Chapter 8: Building Healthy Relationships and Attachment

Complex developmental trauma inevitably disrupts attachment - our capacity to bond with others in relationships that provide comfort, consistency, and security. But earned secure attachment can be cultivated later through new constructive interpersonal experiences.

This chapter explores how to mindfully build healthy relationships that counteract the legacy of early attachment wounds. By incrementally taking risks, communicating vulnerably, and establishing boundaries, we relearn connection. We release past projections to relate to others as they are. Our openness expands.

While the process has challenges, human closeness represents our greatest potential. From brokenness, Trust and love can slowly grow.

Attachment Wounds

Early violation and neglect sabotage forming coherent working models of relationships as sources of safety and responsiveness. Without reliable nurturing caretakers, basic trust fails to develop. Fear directs connection unconsciously.

Common attachment wounds stemming from complex trauma include:

- Difficulty feeling safe and soothed around others

- Compromised ability to articulate needs and set interpersonal boundaries

- Disorganized internal working models flitting between anxious, avoidant, fearful

- Unconcious relationship templates based in domination, exploitation, rescue

- Projecting traumatizers onto new people leading to learned helplessness or lashing out

- Suppressing genuine self to appease, perform, evade danger

- Social perception skewed towards detecting threats versus reading positive cues

- Yearning for affection but panic when emotionally intimate or dependent

- Isolating to prevent feared engulfment or rejection

Yet earned secure attachment is possible through new relational experiences. The brain remains plastic for bonding across the lifespan. Trust can be constructed even when early foundations cracked.

Stages of Healthy Bonding

Constructing a coherent secure attachment style as an adult after childhood relational trauma requires moving sequentially through stages:

Safety – Ensure protection and consistently tend to basic needs without harm, neglect, or boundary violations. Test waters slowly.

Reliability – Demonstrate predictable attunement, empathy, and reunions after separations. Keep word. Build track record through small interactions.

Vulnerability – Share incremental risky disclosures and feelings. Receive grace. Try out trust while maintaining safety nets.

Assertiveness – Once safety and trust established, practice expressing needs, preferences, disagreements. Resolve conflicts rather than withdraw or placate.

Interdependence – Attain ability for closeness without losing autonomous self. Be intimate while maintaining boundaries. Give and receive care.

New narrative – Accumulated experiences allow updating unconscious relationship templates and projections to reflect current healthy dynamics, not just past violations.

With time and trial and error, we integrate new learning that people can be present, attuned, comforting. Our openness returns.

Finding Safe People

Establishing security internally makes us discerning when seeking external attachments. We no longer desperately accept anyone showing interest, nor rigidly reject all out of fear. Through mindful trial and error, we identify those offering authentic nurturing.

Some tips on finding safe people:

- Start slowly sharing surface-level social activities to gently test reliability over time before pursuing deeper one-on-one vulnerable bonding.

- Ask for support around a minor challenging issue to assess if they can respect boundaries and respond helpfully when you need care. How do they handle your pain?

- Gauge if they seem reasonably stable and consistent in mood and commitment in low-risk situations first. Build a track record of small trust.

- Notice your inner signals of safety and enjoyment when together versus activated trauma responses. Healthy relating elicits calm.

- Pay close attention to whether they take initiative and invest in planning contact. Relationships should not feel one-sided.

- Do they apologize for unintended misattunements? Make repairs? Accept responsibility? Work through difficulties?

- When saying no to a request, are they able to accept your boundary vs. becoming aggressive or passive aggressive?

Take time assessing potential friends and partners before deepening intimacy. Healthy relating is reciprocal, responsively attuned and resilient through conflicts.

Healthy Communication

Replacing dysfunctional communication patterns conditioned by early trauma requires learning and practicing new skills like emotional literacy, boundary setting, conflict resolution, and compromising. With commitment, neural pathways rewire through repeated practice.

Some components of healthy communication include:

Emotional literacy – Name your feelings and needs rather than expecting others to mind-read them. Start sentences with "I feel..." rather than "You make me..." Taking ownership of inner states prevents projection.

Active listening – When others share feelings, reflect back compassionately what you heard before responding. Ensure you understand. Ask clarifying questions.

Boundary setting – Politely decline any interaction you don't want or request behavior adjustments using "I" language about your limits. You never owe others compliance.

Collaborative conflict - Raise issues calmly, hear other's perspective, identify mutual needs, brainstorm solutions, compromise. No verbal attacks or stonewalling. Take breaks if agitated.

Repair attempts – Offer sincere apologies for inevitable misattunements. Rupture is normal. Make amends to restore connection through talking, acts of service or gestures.

Tolerating imperfection – Let go unrealistic expectations demanding perfection in self or others. We all make mistakes. Forgive yourself and others while still taking responsibility.

Speaking plainly – Don't expect others to mind-read cues. Directly yet kindly state what you mean without dropping hints or passive aggression. Reduce frustration through forthrightness.

Practice conversation skills even when challenging. In relearning healthy relating, progress outpaces perfection. We get there through small steps.

Developing Assertiveness

Assertiveness involves standing up for yourself and your values in ways that are straightforward, calm, and respectful of others. It replaces trauma patterns of aggression or passive compliance in aiming to reach mutual understanding.

Some components of assertive relating include:

- **StatIng needs simply** – Without demanding, make direct clear requests for what would help you feel cared for using "I" language about your experience.

- **Establishing boundaries** - Politely decline requests or behavior that overextends your energy, time or values. You never owe others compliance. Just be kind in protecting yourself.

- **Expressing valid criticism** – Share feedback about problematic behaviors without character attacks. Use "I" language about your feelings and effects on you. Allow others dignity.

- **Holding others accountable** – Require friends or partners to take concrete responsibility for harmful actions without excuses. Let natural consequences motivate change. Don't enable.

- **Voicing reasonable objections** – If suggestions or group norms trouble you, respectfully explain your differing perspective. Agree to disagree when needed. Silencing your inner voice breeds resentment.

- **Open negotiation** – When disagreements happen, identify mutual needs and brainstorm solutions both people feel okay with. Be creative versus oppositional.

- **Managing conflict** - Master calming yourself before discussing ruptures. Then re-engage vulnerably. No verbal assaults or emotional withdrawal. Stay present through the process.

Relating assertively builds self-trust and allows intimacy with autonomy. You can be direct without requiring defensiveness. There are solutions meeting both people's core needs.

Developing Trusting Relationships

Relearning to trust others enough to receive care and show vulnerable pieces of yourself requires taking graduated relational risks over time. We slowly expand our window of safety through corrective experiences.

Some suggestions for fostering trust wisely:

- Start slowly sharing interests, thoughts, and feelings on more superficial topics to build a foundation. No major personal disclosures initially.

- Test reliability by sharing a minor worry or asking for small help. Do they respond with care versus dismissal?

- Watch for signs of consistent attentiveness like remembering details you mentioned or noticing your shifting moods. This indicates dependability.

- Request they maintain confidentiality with private information you share as you open up more over time. Ensure they honor this.

- Share slight vulnerabilities and observe responses. Are they empathic? Do they open up similarly or stay closed off and critical?

- Check in with yourself after interactions. Do you feel soothed and more connected or activated and distrustful? Inner signals reveal safety.

- Risk expressing appropriate needs. Are they willing to adjust caretaking to your requests? Can you collaborate?

With wisdom, we give new relationships time earning our faith inch by inch. We can gradually trust again after trauma's violations. Patience allows wholeness.

Healthy Boundaries

Boundaries involve maintaining a clear sense of identity within relationships - knowing where you end and others begin. They prevent the enmeshment and loss of self common after childhood trauma. Boundaries foster secure interdependence.

Some examples of healthy relationship boundaries:

- Not abandoning your routines, values, or interests to excessively accommodate someone else's preferences

- Asking that friends respect your needed quiet or alone time to preserve energy

- Expecting others keep your private disclosures confidential and not share without permission

- Choosing not to tolerate abuse, manipulation, or unhealthy behaviors from others

- Limiting time spent listening to someone else's constant negativity or problems

- Refusing to take responsibility for someone else's emotions or try to "fix" them

- Politely saying no to requests you genuinely do not want to fulfill - no excuses needed

- Not sharing intimate details too quickly before establishing someone's trustworthiness

- Following through on threatened reasonable consequences if others violate clear boundaries

What distinguishes healthy boundaries is maintaining self-care without attempting to control others. We set limits while allowing autonomy.

Grieving Attachment Losses

A pivotal part of recovering from developmental attachment wounds involves allowing space for grief over trust and nurturance lost prematurely. What could not be mourned fully when young remained frozen until we are emotionally equipped later to process it.

Some suggestions for grieving attachment losses:

- Find a therapist or support group willing to bear witness and hold space for this primal sadness and anger. censor

- Express feelings through crying, journaling, artwork, music or other creative forms of release. Let the tears flow.

- Consider writing unsent letters to absent, neglectful, or abusive caretakers. Name the ways you needed them that they failed to provide.

- Through ritual, officially release fantasies that unresponsive caregivers will somehow become present and attuned now. Hold a relinquishment ceremony.

- Take time to comfort your inner child still carrying attachment pain. Provide the soothing and empathy you needed. Dialogue with this part compassionately.

- Spend periods processing grief each day to allow full experiencing. Expect intense waves to come and go. Ride them out.

- Remind yourself daily you are worthy of nurturance. Challenge old programs of inadequacy. You are enough.

- Reflect on any positive childhood attachment experiences you did receive. There were likely some sources of felt security.

While we cannot change the past, we can heal from it by fully grieving violation of emotional bonds meant to bring safety and comfort. We release old wounds from their grip.

Common Relational Patterns

We commonly recreate childhood attachment dynamics unconsciously through familiar but dysfunctional relating styles. Recognizing these patterns is key to interrupting trauma reenactment.

Codependence - Excessive caretaking, enmeshment, neglecting self to gain approval, intense anxiety when apart. Tries to force intimacy.

Avoidance - Extreme independence, unwillingness to show neediness, distancing self when emotions arise. Intimacy feels too risky.

Rescuer-Victim - Getting drawn into unstable "helping" dynamics recreating childhood chaos. Never feeling worthy without saving someone.

Clinging - Preoccupied worrying a partner will leave. Jealous. Makes constant demands for time and reassurance. Anxiety spirals.

Sabotage - Pushing away loved ones through criticism, chaos, substance abuse or neglect due to fear of abandonment once attached. Self-fulfilling prophecy.

Idealization - Placing partners on a pedestal then devaluing them when the illusion cracks. Black and white relating. Intensity fades.

Emotionalcutoff - Fear of enmeshment leads distancing from anyone who starts expecting emotional intimacy and support. Isolating to avoid engulfment.

Noting unhealthy patterns renders them conscious so new choices can override old programming. We pursue consistency, reciprocity and compassion.

Supportive Friendships

Nurturing platonic friendships help instill secure attachment by offering consistency, companionship, and caretaking outside of romance. They model healthy relating patterns for when we are ready for deeper partnership intimacy.

Some hallmarks of true friendship include:

- Mutual comfort being authentic, silly, imperfect without needing to perform

- Laughing together about shared interests, memories, and inside jokes

- Sincere listening and emotional support during hard times

- Celebrating each other's wins, talents, and accomplishments

- Forgiving mistakes and oversights quickly

- Communicating needs without shame, judgement or extremes

- Compassion for each other's quirks and past wounds

- Occasional physical affection, if welcomed, like hugs, hand holding, pats on the back

- Directness combined with gentleness when sharing constructive feedback

Friends become chosen family. Through consistently showing up for each other, bonds of trust grow. We naturally learn to rely on and be relied upon. It feels safe.

Navigating Conflict

Disagreements and ruptures in relationships are normal. How we navigate conflict determines whether trust ultimately strengthens or breaks. With compassion, ruptures become openings for deeper mutual understanding and intimacy.

Some principles for successful conflict resolution include:

- Tolerance - Accepting frustration, hurt, and anger will sometimes arise in caring relationships. This is natural and expected. Stay present.

- Ownership - Speaking for how you uniquely experience and interpret disputes. Using "I" language versus blaming.

- Listening - Making space to understand the other's perspective with openness before responding. Suspending assumptions. Asking clarifying questions.

- Vulnerability - Being honest about underlying feelings and attachment wounds history may have imprinted that heighten reactivity. Taking appropriate responsibility for overreactions while acknowledging root causes.

- Repair attempts - Sincerely apologizing for any misattunement. Trying to remedy through action, not just words. Making amends.

- Compromise - Identifying fair solutions that honor both party's core needs. Giving the benefit of doubt and meeting halfway.

- Forgiveness - Focusing on each other's positive intent once tensions calm. Releasing grudges. Rebuilding connection.

- Education - Reading resources together on healthy conflict resolution skills. Improving through behavioral changes.

With maturity and practice, rupture leads to greater closeness. We grow most handling hard conversations with courage and care for the relationship beyond the argument.

Letters to Your Future Self

A powerful exercise as you progress in relational recovery from complex trauma is writing letters of wisdom, reassurance, and guidance to your future self when you are struggling. You become your own secure attachment figure through loving self-talk.

Consider including:

- Affirmation of how far you have come already and the strengths you posses to keep healing, even during crisis moments when this feels impossible. You endured so much to already be where you are.

- Reminders that painful relationship patterns and emotions are normal following childhood trauma. You are not defective. Have self-compassion regarding symptoms.

- Encouragement that with support, time, and practice, you can and will build trust and intimacy with safe people at your own pace. This part of you remains undamaged.

- What you most needed to hear during painful relational moments in your past. Offer that nurturance to yourself internally now.

- Ways you learned to calm yourself, tolerate distress, or take protective steps when relationships become chaotic or scary. You have resources.

- Insights on underlying core needs motivating maladaptive behaviors. Interpret own actions compassionately.

- Affirmations of your inherent worthiness of love, belonging, and support. You are doing the best you can. Just keep going.

During flashbacks or relationship conflicts, literally read letters you wrote reassuring your heart with wisdom perspective and care. Take in needed comfort.

Spiritual Connection

Whether religious or secular, cultivating a sense of spirituality, meaning, and connection to forces greater than the individual self provides a secure relational base. This compensates for early falta of consistent human attachment and instills existential coherence.

Potential avenues for spiritual attachment include:

- Traditional religious involvement such as church, temple, or mosque

- Connection to nature and the beauty of the Universe

- Volunteering to help others as humanitarian "calling"

- Creative immersion through art, music, writing as transcendence

- Meditation, or mindfulness practices

- Seeking truth through philosophy and insightful dialogues

- Therapeutic soul work with guides like shamanism or Jungian analysis

- Belonging to groups organized around ethics and social justice

- Learning from meaningful rituals, texts, poetry and traditions

Whatever form resonates, we yearn for purpose outside ourselves. When human support falters, spiritual connection sustains hope. We recall we are part of something larger.

Animal Companions

Caring attachments with animal companions provides significant therapeutic benefit for complex trauma recovery. Pets model unconditional acceptance, consistent responsiveness, calming touch, and honest communication lacking in traumatic human relationships. They make safe conduits for vulnerability.

Research on benefits confirms pets help:

- Regulate emotion - Stroking animals releases oxytocin, endorphins, and lowers stress hormones

- Build secure attachment - Pets offer constant nurturance and physical affection

- Boost mood - Playing and cuddling pets stimulates feel-good brain chemicals

- Increase mindfulness - Their needs require present-focused caretaking

- Reduce loneliness - Nonverbal companionship when isolated

- Instill meaning - Necessity of their caretaking provides purpose

- Encourage activity - Dog walking fosters helpful daily routines

- Lower anxiety - Stroking animals has centering effect on nervous system

- Improve health - Lowered blood pressure, heart rate, and pain levels

If possible, caring daily for an animal companion provides unconditional love needed to counteract relational trauma. Their sensitivity helps repair human disconnection.

Healthy Physical Contact

When early touch was unsafe, chaotic, or neglectfully absent, survivors often avoid or desperately pursue it seeking control. Finding healthy physical intimacy requires reconditioning through gradually building positive tactile experiences with safe others.

Some suggestions for cultivating healthy physical closeness include:

- Set the pace. Never feel rushed into forms of touch that activationsurvival reactions. Freeze, flee, or submit responses reveal it is too much too soon. Wait until emotions settle.

- Start slowly with minimal doses of safe nurturing contact like handholding, pats on the shoulder, brief hugs, holding pets. Slowly increase ability to tolerate affection.

- Notice physical tension arising. Keep breath relaxed in belly and eyes softly gazing to remain present rather than dissociating.

- Soothe inner child reactions through internally reassuring "I am safe now" while receiving caring touch. Infuse compassion into the present.

- Tell trusted friends exactly when touch feels comforting versus triggering. They will adjust accordingly. Identify safe people willing to re-build positive associations.

- Take regular comforting mini-breaks alone if interactions involve prolonged eye contact, social efforts. Prevent going into overdrive.

- Request friends model giving platonic nurturing touch through massage, hugs, handholding. Practice reciprocating at your own pace.

With time, caring physical affection can feel warm versus threatening. We unravel knots slowly but surely through replacing past pain with present peace.

Reflections

- What new relational skills outlined in this chapter resonate most with your growth edges in recovery? Where do you want to build capacity?

- Reflect on moments recently you handled relationships in healthier more conscious ways than you may have in the past before recovery. Appreciate evidence of progress.

- Consider ways spirituality or commitment to values larger than the self could help stabilize and soothe you when interpersonal ruptures occur.

- What inner work around attachment wounds still feels needed? What internalized templates or

Chapter 9: Rediscovering Purpose and Meaning

Healing from complex PTSD involves reclaiming a sense of meaning, agency, hope and purpose after adversity threatened to extinguish our spark. We nourish neglected parts of self, pursue passions, and contribute to the world from our wounds and wisdom.

When past pain defined existence, creating rich purpose liberates life's potential going forward. Our compass resets from surviving to thriving. What fulfills you? What communities and causes ignite commitment? You have the opportunity to determine the path forward.

This chapter explores pathways for rediscovering personal meaning and direction after trauma. We reignite intrinsic motivation and passions once suppressed. Creative action aligns existence with values. We redeem the past by allowing it to fuel a purposeful future.

Reflecting on Meaning

Healing complex developmental trauma centers on transforming our relationship to the past. This involves making sense of it rather than being defined by it. Reflection questions can catalyze insight about overarching meaning.

Some examples include:

- How did my journey shape my character and values? What matters most to me now as a result?

- What intrinsic strengths did I discover in myself through facing adversity that I can build on?

- How did trauma shape my sensitivity, empathy and insights about human nature in positive ways?

- What new priorities or perspectives emerged about life's meaning from glimpsing darkness?

- How did my wounds give rise to passions and creativity as outlets for pain?

- What social causes or humanitarian impulses now compel me to help others based on what I endured?

- How did adversity deepen my spirituality or faith in ways that now comfort and guide me?

- What wisdom can I pass on to others struggling that would provide hope and direction?

Making meaning is an ongoing process of extracting wisdom from life's complexities. We redeem suffering by interpreting it as teachers meant to develop our souls.

Post-Traumatic Growth

Suffering can give rise to post-traumatic growth - psychological thriving and enhanced functioning from contending with chronic illness, loss, abuse, disaster, or adversity. Growth naturally occurs when trauma is processed according to researchers.

Common areas encompassed by post-traumatic growth include:

- Deepened spirituality and appreciation for life's fragility

- Expanded compassion, altruism, and dedication to helping fellow survivors

- Improved personal strength, resilience, confidence, and power

- Changed priorities and values about what matters most

- Closer relationships with those who proved supportive during hardship

- Greater vulnerability, authenticity, and emotional expressiveness

- Renewed passion, creativity, sense of possibility about life

- Emergence of new possible directions and purpose

With compassion, time, and work, we turn wounds into wisdom. Our broken places become passageways to purpose. An indestructible soul learns to shine brighter.

Reclaiming Joy

Recovering joy, delight, play, and fun often feels challenging after past trauma conditioned depression, hypervigilance, and disconnection from the body. But incorporating small pleasures into daily life proves deeply restorative. It reminds us we deserve to feel lightness.

Some simple ways to welcome more joy include:

- Make a list of childhood activities that brought you pleasure, play, and laughter. Begin re-engaging those inner parts through adult versions.

- Spend regular time outdoors immersing in the sights, sounds, and sensations of nature. Allow its aliveness to resonate through you.

- Create a playlist of upbeat, happy songs to dance, sing along, or move freely to. Let go in the rhythms.

- Watch comedy movies or shows. Let yourself belly laugh.

- Try creative arts like finger painting, Lego structures, coloring books. Take joy in free play.

- Share jokes and funny stories with trusted friends. Humor bonds and releases tension.

- Indulge your senses with scents, textures, sounds, and foods you enjoy. Don't deny yourself small pleasures.

- Recall recent moments when you felt spontaneous delight. What catalyzed this? Seek out more such moments.

Though shadowed by adversity's weight, we gently re-ignite awareness of beauty surrounding us everywhere. Delight lives in exquisite ordinary moments we fail to notice when suffering preoccupies. Wake up to wonder. It heals.

Exploring Passions

Suppressing creative energies and passions to survive often results in depression, emptiness, and lack of direction. Reawakening intrinsic interests and motivations brings vitality. It connects to our essence beneath trauma's weight. What stirs you?

Here are some reflections to help identify hidden passions:

- What drew your curiosity, delight, and engagement as a child before outside pressures shaped your course? What came naturally?

- When do you lose track of time or become immersed in positive flow states? What activities absorb your focus?

- What topics could you talk enthusiastically about for hours? What leaves you feeling energized?

- What activities, skill development, exchange of knowledge, or self-expression ignite a passionate spark within you? What brings you a profound sense of vitality?

- What interests did you suppress or abandon due to lack of resources, confidence or support? What dreams hold allure?

- What social causes or injustices ignite your outrage and action?

- What quotes, lyrics, poems, or stories deeply resonate? What truths ring for you?

- If you had unlimited time, freedom, and encouragement, what would you passionately pursue or create?

Reawakening passion for living replenishes us. What enlivens your spirit most? Pursue it without guilt. Your joy contributes light.

Clarifying Priorities

Healing complex trauma opens space to thoughtfully craft a values-based life aligned with our needs. We take back agency to chart a conscious course rather than just reactively surviving. Clarifying priorities lends direction.

Some reflection questions to help identify core priorities:

- When reflecting on your life in its later stages, what holds the greatest significance for you? How would you prefer to have utilized your time?

- What types of activities leave you feeling nourished versus depleted? What rhythms of engagement work best?

- As you reflect on the later stages of your life, what holds the greatest significance for you? How do you envision your ideal use of time?

- What touchstones guide you through uncertainty: ethics, spiritual truths, compassion, creativity?

- What relationships feel truly life-giving and accepting of your whole self as is? Prioritize these.

- Where do you still feel inner conflict or misalignment between values and actions? How could you realign?

- What aspects of life feel non-negotiable to protect? What trade-offs are you unwilling to make?

- What fears hold you back from boldly pursuing dreams? How could you move forward despite vulnerabilities?

Healing means living who you were before trauma interfered with the seed of your becoming. Listen within for what wants flowering in this next stage.

Crafting a New Narrative

We make sense of life through the internal narratives and dominant stories we adopt about our existence. Trauma often creates themes of damage, powerlessness, and hopelessness. We can consciously re-author empowering narratives.

Some examples of positive life narratives:

- My suffering makes me wiser and more compassionate. I will use it to help others heal.

- What happened to me does not define my potential or essence. I choose how to let it shape me.

- I am the hero, not victim, of my story. My quest makes me stronger.

- Darkness helped me appreciate light. Struggling expanded my capacity for joy.

- My life has meaning and gifts waiting to be discovered each day. There are always second chances.

- I trust in larger unfolding forces of healing. My role is showing up open to growth.

- I am the creator of a meaningful life. My narrative remains receptive to hope and the possibility of transformation.

We get to write the remaining chapters. Surviving past pain readied you for whatever comes next. You know how strong you are.

Learning From the Past

While we cannot change what happened, we can choose what we carry forward. Healing involves gleaning wisdom from the past to guide us now without remaining tethered to old stories. We extract lessons while letting go pain.

Some reflection questions:

- What inner strengths and resources did you uncover through surviving adversity that you can build on?

- How did you manage to endure situations through creativity, courage, patience or will? Appreciate these.

- When things were hardest, what healthy comforts and coping strategies sustained you? Carry these with you.

- What positive sources of support or inspiration made a difference along the way? Hold onto these.

- How did struggle ripen your compassion, character, and priorities about what matters most?

- What new possibilities or passions emerged through having to heal and recreate?

- How are you wiser and more grateful after being tested? What still feels precious?

We honor past hardship by refusing to waste the growth it demanded. We painfully earned this wisdom and self-knowledge. It is now an inner light guiding us.

Writing Your Own Story

Literally narrating your personal story through journaling or memoir writing helps order scattered traumatic memories into an empowering testimony. We become the narrator of our own journey. Writing down and sharing stories organizes experience and fosters post-traumatic growth according to researchers.

Some tips if you feel called to write your story:

- Focus on how you survived, escaped, overcame adversity. Highlight courage.

- Illustrate how you changed and grew stronger through struggling. Share insights gained.

- Vividly depict obstacles overcome. Use metaphor and imagery.

- Balance darkness with light. Convey sources of hope, beauty, comfort, and human kindness that sustained you.

- Portray yourself as hero on a journey, not just passive victim. You showed strength and agency.

- Allow inspiration, humor, and positive memories to permeate the narrative. Wholeness includes joy and suffering.

- Express gratitude for those who helped along the way. Acknowledge supporters.

- Celebrate the phases of progress in healing. Convey optimism about the future.

- Consider publishing your story or excerpts to help fellow survivors feel less alone. Our wounds make us kindred.

You lived a story worth telling and hearing. Through expressing your truth, you triumph.

Ritualizing Transformation

Rituals give structure to celebrating change, passage from one life season to the next, or mourning one aspect of self to welcome another. Ceremony facilitates internal shifts. Consider creating rituals to honor your healing.

Some examples of meaningful rituals include:

- Creating an altar space with items symbolically representing your journey

- Crafting a healing mandala from scenes in nature or your imagination

- Holding a ceremony to burn old belongings representing the past

- Gathering friends to share readings, music, dance, or food that narrate chapters of your story

- Immersing yourself in water to symbolize cleansing pain, being reborn

- Taking a pilgrimage to a symbolic place signifying transition

- Writing down negative self-beliefs and burying or burning them

- Sharing your testimony with a supportive community

- Composing a song, poem, or piece of art capturing your evolution

- Planting a tree to represent your growth toward the sun

Rituals provide structure for mystic processes of death and rebirth as we shed old skin. We honor inner transitions.

Volunteering and Service

Contributing time and care to causes aligned with your values represents a powerful path to renewed meaning and purpose. Service offers ways to transform pain into good. When we support others, our own suffering gains context. We realize our experiences equip us uniquely to help in ways that provide fulfillment.

Some meaningful ways to contribute may include:

- Staffing crisis lines to offer support you gained through your journey

- Sharing your story at support groups and centers to help fellow survivors

- Lobbying for legislation and policies related to trauma prevention and support

- Fundraising for research and access to trauma therapies

- Serving as a peer mentor for those healing from similar issues

- Donating time or goods to women's shelters, orphanages, recovery programs

- Fostering rescue animals who often endured their own trauma

- Volunteering skills, resources to organizations advancing social justice

- Creating spaces, events, songs, works of art that inspire hope and strength

- Simple daily actions like smiling at strangers, helping neighbors, listening generously

Healing through service allows us to take the compassion we cultivated through suffering and share it directly to bless wounded souls still finding their way. We pass along the light.

Continuing Education

Immersing yourself in learning environments related to trauma, creativity, spirituality, psychology, philosophy, social justice or other domains that inspire you fosters a sense of momentum. Forward movement is healing. Allow curiosity to guide your choices.

Some educational pathways to consider include:

- Classes at community colleges, universities, teaching institutes

- Workshops, conferences, seminars, retreats

- Certification programs and trainings

- Peer support groups focused on growth

- Online courses, podcasts, workbooks, videos

- Private tutoring or mentoring in an area of interest from an expert

- Discussion and book groups exploring meaningful ideas

- Attending lectures, presentations, and talks from innovators

- Travel experiences introducing new cultures, people, perspectives

- Self-guided reading, research, and creative projects

Let education occupy spaces once filled by trauma. An open, curious mind welcomes inspiration and purpose. You rediscover meaning through fresh knowledge. Keep planting seeds.

Expressing Creativity

Engaging creative arts, hobbies, and innovations provides among the most direct pathways to post-traumatic growth. The brain and body heal through right-brained processes that structure inner chaos into tangible form. Making beauty from pain redeems suffering.

Some expressive modalities to explore include:

- Visual arts like painting, drawing, sculpture, quilting, collage, photography, woodworking

- Writing poetry, prose, memoirs, stories, journaling, lyric analysis

- Playing, composing music and songs through voice, instruments, technology

- Healing modalities like aromatherapy, flower essences, herbalism

- Exploring new ways of looking through cosmology, birds, stargazing, microscopy

- Building things through construction, electronics, robotics, carpentry, auto repairs

- Cooking, baking, mixology, and infusing art into culinary pursuits

- Growing gardens, caring for plants, ikebana flower arranging

- Sewing, jewelry making, soap crafting, candle making, knitting, textiles

Your unique imagination has power to reorder chaos into something beautiful which structures grief. Let it flow freely. The process of creating heals.

Flow States

Flow describes optimal states of creative immersion where we feel carried in purposeful action, losing track of time. Pursuing talent-aligned challenges with focus fosters flow. Trauma impedes it. Restoring activities that breed joyful flow states recovers aliveness.

Some examples of flow activities include:

- Making art, cooking, photography, poetry absorbed in the process

- Playing instruments, singing, dancing with senses immersed

- Sports like running, skiing, surfing, climbing invoking adrenaline and laser attention

- Losing self fully in social dancing, musical jam sessions, acting improv

- Becoming one with nature while hiking, gardening, swimming in the sea

- Tinkering, building, repairing, restoring vehicles or crafts with full focus

- Playing challenging games requiring intense strategy both mental like chess and physical

- Learning new skills that stretch current competence like languages or coding

- Providing complete presence through massage, listening generously, teaching students

- Leading causes selflessly centered on service greater than personal gain

Immersed in flow, trauma's disruptions dissolve as we surrender to joy of inspired action. Time stops. There is only now.

Engaging Communities

Supportive communities help instill meaning through opportunities to share resources, build belonging, and contribute strengths. Isolation activates trauma reactions. Finding our people grounds us.

Some examples of meaningful groups include:

- Spiritual communities like churches, temples, or meditation circles

- Clubs or co-ops organized around hobbies, sports, games, arts

- Volunteer groups mobilizing for social justice causes

- Mutual aid networks providing solidarity and support

- Group therapy, support groups, 12-step meetings

- Co-living communities organized around values

- Online groups of kindred spirits and interests

- Leadership in youth mentoring organizations

- Neighborhood associations strengthening local bonds

- Nonprofit boards supporting life-affirming missions

- Conferences and meet-ups engaging bright minds

Within community, our voice belongs and contributes. Generosity returns generosity. Hard realities feel shared. Together, we create microcosms of the just, equitable, caring world we wish to see.

Mentoring Others

Whether informally or through formal programs, serving as a mentor for youth or fellow survivors brings immense meaning. Drawing from your lived experiences to help guide others through struggle is privilege. Your pain can illuminate their path.

Some benefits of mentoring include:

- Passing hard-won strengths and wisdom forward to uplift others

- Providing living proof that healing and thriving are possible after trauma

- Helping fellow survivors and youth feel less alone in their darkness

- Developing self-efficacy as your support makes a tangible difference

- Gaining perspective from those with fresh eyes on ways you overcame obstacles

- Feeling the meaningfulness of your journey through improving other lives

- Learning invaluable lessons yourself about resilience from those you mentor

- Processing your own experiences more deeply as you formulate guidance

All of us have known darkness. That darkness is the very source that allows us to share light. Through giving what we needed, we receive all over again tenfold.

Cultivating Gratitude

Intentionally noticing and appreciating the good surrounding us represents a simple yet powerful practice for transforming trauma's legacies of feeling deprived, bitter, or pessimistic. Gratitude breeds joy. It lifts eyes from lack

Chapter 10: Practicing Mindfulness and Emotional Regulation

The capacity to mindfully observe experiences without judgment or impulsive reaction represents a pivotal skill for overcoming complex trauma. By noticing thoughts, emotions, and sensations simply as passing phenomena, we can respond thoughtfully even when triggered.

This chapter explores how mindfulness practices build distress tolerance, emotion regulation, empathy, and secure attention. We anchor in each moment instead of reliving the past or fearing the future. Equanimity becomes possible even amidst inner storms.

While challenging at first, meditation and other mindful approaches retrain attention and openness to foster post-traumatic growth. They return us from states of chronic emergency to our center of wise compassion. Be patient. Mindfulness builds slowly but powerfully.

The Mindfulness Foundation

Mindfulness simply means paying purposeful nonjudgmental attention to unfolding experience in the present moment. It involves tuning into thoughts, physical sensations, and emotions with gentle curiosity rather than criticism.

Key concepts include:

- Noticing external stimuli through the senses - sounds, smells, tastes, touch, sights

- Observing internal sensations in the body - tightness, adrenaline, pain

- Witnessing thoughts and emotions arising and passing without believing or acting on them

- Recognizing stimuli as neutral data versus good or bad, dangerous or safe

- Accepting all input without attachment, suppression or escalating stories

- Gently returning attention when it wanders to additional stimuli arising each moment

Mindfulness builds the muscle of focused equanimity amidst all experience. It empowers conscious response versus reflexive reaction.

Benefits of Mindfulness

Extensive research confirms mindfulness meditation physically changes the brain, reducing trauma-induced amygdala reactivity while thickening prefrontal regions that govern executive functioning. With practice, tangible benefits naturally arise:

- Increased distress tolerance and emotion regulation

- Heightened concentration and cognitive flexibility

- Expanded empathy, compassion, insight into self and others

- Calmer, more present, emotionally balanced state

- Release of trauma stored physically in the body

- Deepened ability to resolve complex problems

- Freedom from reactive patterns and auto-pilot behaviors

- Improved sleep and lowered impulsiveness

- Strengthened immune function and reduced inflammation

- Greater access to inner wisdom beyond stories and judgments

- Perspective on thoughts as passing mental events rather than truth or directives

Mindfulness results from disciplined mental training, not just hoping for benefits. But this training powerfully improves lives.

Focused Attention Practice

A basic mindfulness exercise for those new to meditation involves training concentration through anchoring attention on a single chosen focus like the breath. Each time the mind wanders, we gently return it. This builds capacity for present-moment focus.

Try this classic focused attention practice:

- Assume a stable, comfortable posture with eyes closed or resting unfocused on a single point

- Turn awareness to physical sensations of breathing, concentrating on the steady inflow and outflow

- Let breath flow naturally without attempting to adjust it

- When thoughts, feelings or other sensations arise, simply note "thinking" or "sensing", then return focus to the breath

- If mind wanders repeatedly, patiently keep redirecting to the "anchor" of felt sensations of breathing

- When a wandering or distracting experience arises, avoid self-blame. This is natural. Simply return to the breath.

- After 15-30 minutes, gently open eyes and reflect on the ebb and flow of attention. With compassion, commit to daily practice.

Discipline builds inner calm not grasped at but cultivated through letting go distractions that control our consciousness. We rediscover centeredness.

Mindfulness of the Body

Since trauma manifests physically through chronic hyperarousal, practicing mindfulness of body sensations proves stabilizing. We survey our inner landscape with compassion rather than judgment.

Try this awareness of body practice:

- Sit or lie comfortably, tuning into physical sensations from head to toe without trying to change them

- Start by simply feeling the weight of your body being affected by gravity. Sense your flesh, bones and mass.

- Bring friendly awareness to sensations in each part of your body sequentially - legs, arms, hands, torso, shoulders, neck, head.

- Notice any areas of tightness, looseness, twitching, pulsing, heat, numbness. Breathe into these places.

- With openness, become aware of pain or emotions held in the body without needing resolution. Allow them to just be as sensations.

- If areas feel numb, see if you can gently encourage warmth and aliveness to return through breath. But accept blockages when present.

- Relax into natural rhythm of the body without judgment or need to control. Get curious about its inner workings.

- Appreciate the wondrous ways your physical form sustains you. Send it gratitude.

By making peace with our body's manifestations, we stop fighting the present moment. Our bodies unfurl into alignment.

Mindfulness of Emotions

Beyond physical sensations, mindfulness helps us relate differently to emotions, no longer being flooded away by them. We hold feelings in compassionate awareness, honoring but not unleashing them blindly.

Practice mindful noting of emotions this way:

- When strong emotions arise like anger, sadness, joy or anxiety, pause reactive habits.

- Without judgment, mentally name the emotion you are experiencing. Label it compassionately. "Here is grief", "This is frustration".

- Watch how sensations manifest this emotion in your body. Where do you feel it? How does it make your stomach, heart, throat feel? Stay present.

- Notice if labeling the emotion begins to create some space around it, letting it unfold versus becoming it. You have awareness larger than any single emotion.

- Reflect briefly on what thought patterns may have stimulated the arising of this emotion. But do not get lost in stories. Return to the feeling itself.

- Allow the natural intensity of emotion to crest, stay present, and eventually pass like a wave. Do not amplify storylines about why it lingers. Just breathe.

- After reflecting, consciously redirect focus to your next breath, filling your lungs fully. Continue meditating.

We stop drowning in emotions by learning to float along their waves. We strengthen equanimity in their midst.

Working with Difficult Emotions

Certain emotions like rage, terror, shame, or despair challenge mindfulness capacity. But relating to them with radical acceptance versus rejection fosters integration. We heal through opening, not avoiding.

Some tips for mindfully transforming difficult emotions:

- Get grounded first in your body through feeling gravity, your feet on the floor. Reconnect to stable surroundings.

- Name the emotion and find where you distinctly feel it in your body - fists, throat, stomach. Do not judge or amplify these sensations.

- Visualize painful emotions like storm clouds passing through the open sky of your awareness. You remain still, observing but not inundated.

- Mentally scan your body to relax tightened areas through soft exhales. Pain cannot persist when you stop feeding it with resistance.

- Say to yourself "This too shall pass" recognizing the impermanence of inner states. You've gotten through this before. This time will also end.

- Thank emotions for trying to protect you. Affirm you have adult resources now that make destructive reactions unnecessary.

- Allow healthy tears to release old sorrows entangled with this feeling. Let it flow through you with compassion.

- Remind yourself "I am not this emotion. I am the awareness containing it". You remain whole beyond any single feeling.

Through unconditional presence, even the darkest emotions begin dispersing light. We hold pain so it may transform.

Mindfulness of Thoughts

Much suffering springs from believing thoughts as absolute truth rather than passing mental phenomena. Mindfulness helps dis-identify from unhelpful stories as we learn to watch thoughts arise and pass without attachment.

Practice mindful noting of thoughts through:

- Silently labeling thoughts as "planning", "judging", "worrying" as they flow by without suppressing or following them

- Noting qualities like chaos, looping, hostility, fear, attachment that characterize trauma thought patterns

- Scrambling the literal content of upsetting thoughts like visualizing them jumbled, blurred, scrambled as letters

- Saying "thank you mind" as we notice it fulfilling its role without identifying with unhelpful thoughts

- Visualizing thoughts as clouds morphing into new shapes, leaves floating down a stream. They come and go.

- Setting a timer during meditation for 5 minutes. When it rings, notice how many needless thoughts passed through. This illustrates their ephemerality.

- Getting curious about which situations and moods correlate with increased negative thought patterns. Without judgment, reflect why.

- Affirming "thoughts will come and go but I remain" to build identity separate from transient mental chatter

We cannot stop birds of thought from flying by overhead. But we can refuse to feed and follow them. Watch thought clouds pass through your sky.

Self-Compassion Break

When trauma gets triggered, intentionally cultivating self-compassion through verbal affirmations, soothing touch, and caring imagery grounds us in safety. Being kind toward ourselves in hard moments proves deeply stabilizing.

Try taking this 5 minute self-compassion break when trauma responses arise:

- Speak tenderly to yourself, saying, "This is a response to trauma, and it's not your fault. You are safe and cherished in this moment." Address yourself with the kindness you would offer to a distressed child.

- Place hands over heart, feel the contact and warmth. Or gently stroke arms. Send compassion through touch.

- Visualize someone sincerely looking into your eyes with deep understanding and encouragement. Take in their care.

- Recall a moment someone supported you without judgment when struggling. Feel them with you now.

- Mentally state, "I wish to approach this discomfort with compassion and take good care of myself in this moment." Reiterate these soothing affirmations.

- Picture your experience as a crying toddler being lovingly cradled and rocked. Feel her begin to calm.

Treat yourself as you wish someone had when trauma originally overwhelmed your system. The little one within still needs this compassion.

S.T.O.P. Skills

When traumatic reactions build suddenly, this 4-step mindfulness exercise quickly brings equilibrium by pausing reactive habits. STOP stands for:

S - Stop

Pause whatever you are doing. Take a few slow breaths.

T - Take a step back

Notice physical sensations, thoughts, emotions arising without judging them as good or bad. Just witness.

O - Observe

Tune into your body. Feel the points of contact with the ground, chair. Hear ambient sounds around you. Anchor in the present.

P - Proceed mindfully

After centering yourself, consciously choose a wise action aligned with your values.

Making space between stimulus and response empowers freedom to respond mindfully. We pause, reflect, then act from our center.

Mindfulness in Daily Life

The benefits of mindfulness increase the more we integration it into daily functioning versus just occasional formal meditation. Weave purposeful pauses through routine activities.

Some suggestions for informal practice:

- While washing dishes or brushing teeth, tune into sensations of warm water and scrubbing

- Waiting in line, feel the breath's natural rhythm. Soften any impatience.

- Pause before answering emails or texts. Read carefully. Consider kind intentions before reacting.

- Walking outside, notice birdsong, breeze on skin, the colors of the sky

- During conversations, reflect before responding versus thinking ahead while others talk

- Waiting at a red light, relax jaw and shoulders. Breathe. Feel gravity supporting you.

- Eating slowly, focus fully on flavor and textures. Appreciate nourishment.

- Before bed, scan body for any tension to release. Wish your organs peaceful rest.

We naturally open to calm presence by infusing small moments with wakeful awareness. Mindfulness transforms mundane to sacred.

Loving-Kindness Practice

Loving-kindness meditation focuses positive intentions of care, joy, and equanimity first towards self, then gradually wider circles including loved ones, community, strangers, and all beings. This cultivates compassion.

Try this classic loving-kindness practice:

- Start by genuinely desiring peace, joy, and relief from pain for yourself. Say, "May I experience happiness. May I enjoy good health." Recite these uncomplicated statements at a leisurely pace.

- Once you are prepared, imagine a friend or someone dear to you. Convey your hopes for their well-being and happiness by addressing them by name. Say, "May [their name] find peace, and may [their name] be safe and free from suffering."

- Next, picture neutral people like neighbors, acquaintances. Again, repeat caring intentions. "May you dwell in safety. May you be happy."

- Next, send loving-kindness wishes towards difficult individuals. Take a deep breath. "May you find the inner strength to conquer suffering. May you experience love."

- Lastly, send unlimited wishes of goodwill to every living being on Earth. "May all beings around the world be secure, liberated, and at peace."

Regular practice expands our natural empathy to include those most struggling. It reconditions neural pathways for unconditional compassion - the slippery slope to peace.

Walking Meditation

Combining mindfulness with gentle movement integrates body and mind to soothe trauma. Walking meditation allows anchoring in present surroundings and the feet's contact while thoughts flow by. We return from distraction to grounded presence.

Practice walking this way:

- Stand still first, feeling gravity's support. Soften belly. Shoulders back.

- When ready, take an attentive step forward, noting physical sensations in the sole. Feel your heel, then ball of foot, then toes touch the ground.

- With each step, tune into the swinging of your arms, shifting weight, breeze on skin, sounds of birds or traffic. Be here fully.

- If eager to get somewhere, slow down the pace. There is only the present.

- If mind wanders, come back to felt sense of steady feet stepping, cool air, gravity's pull. This moment is enough.

- Appreciate legs' strength. Delight in movement capability.

- At any point, stop and rock or shift weight mindfully before continuing the meditative walk.

Regular walking meditations teach being fully in our bodies, awake to the present. Cares fall away when we enter this flow state. Soon this calm suffuses daily life.

Mindfulness Reminders

Given tendencies for trauma survivors to become lost in past or future worrying, placing daily reminders to anchor back into mindful presence assists recovery. Cues call us back to now.

Some creative mindfulness reminders:

- Notes saying "Breathe" or "Be here now"

- Finger tapping or bracelets that cue noticing sensory input

- Bell sounds on phone reminding to feel gravity, relax shoulders

- Nature photos as smartphone wallpaper

- Desk objects like stones, plants, Zen quotes centering attention

- Timers that chime through the day interrupting autopilot

- Awakening senses by smelling fresh flowers, sipping tea

- Short inspirational verses to repeat when stressed

- Mindfulness apps sending scheduled alerts to stop and breathe

- Alarms for frequent micropauses to check in

- Watch, clock or wristband faced inward to necessitate mindful noticing

The present moment forever awaits our return. Simple cues help interrupt entrenched patterns, opening space for calm presence underlying everything.

Healthy Distraction Skills

When traumatic emotions erupt with overwhelming intensity, temporarily diverting focus can help disarm their spiral until we regain internal balance to address them properly. Healthy distraction builds important distress tolerance.

Some positive ways to distract when spiraling:

- Engrossing activities like cooking, arts and crafts, musical instruments

- Games requiring strategy and focus like puzzles, Tetris, word searches

- Immersive and engaging films, shows, books

- Funny podcasts or uplifting music playlists to lighten heavy moods

- Structured sports like batting cages, wall climbing, running laps

- Volunteering for causes bigger than personal problems

- Organizing clutter or cleaning to instill order externally

- Calling a supportive friend or attending support groups

- Hugging a stuffed animal or petting a soothing animal

- Relaxing guided visualizations for manageable doses of calm

Distraction works best when positively directed versus endless scrolling. We intentionally shift attention to weather inner storms until able to address core wounds skillfully.

Urge Surfing

Cravings and urges often besiege trauma survivors seeking control through destructive impulsive behaviors like binging, substance abuse, gambling or self-harm. Urge surfing allows tolerating these temporary waves skillfully.

Try this 5 step approach:

1. **Mindfulness** - Without judgment, notice and name the rising urge. Accept and allow it to be there without acting immediately. Ride it out.

2. **Urge wave** - Tune into any physical sensations composing the urge. Feel where they manifest in your body like tightness in belly or quickened pulse. Just monitor.

3. **Cresting** - Realize this urge will intensify to a peak before it breaks and dissolves like a wave. You need only withstand the rise, not forever. It will recede every time.

4. **Breathing** - Anchor in your breath without attempting to manipulate it. Feel your lungs fill and empty. Stay anchored in each inhale and exhale as the urge crests.

5. **Affirmation** - Repeat a phrase like "this too shall pass" to reinforce that the urge wave will break. You are stronger than any single fleeting sensation. You can ride it out.

Like a surfer bobbing atop an ocean wave, we regain balance by trusting the ebb and flow of even painful inner states. Change remains ever ongoing if we patiently endure.

Somatic Awareness

Trauma introduces chronic bodily tension and disconnection from internal signals. Somatic mindfulness helps remedy this through tuning into messages from the body and releasing bound energy through sensation.

Some entry points for body awareness include:

Breath - Placing hands on belly and becoming mesmerized by the hypnotic rise and fall with each inhale and exhale

Muscle groups - Systematically tensing and releasing specific areas of face, legs, arms, hands, shoulders, neck, chest. Feel where trauma got stuck. Soften chronically contracted areas.

Weight - Tuning into gravity's pull on your mass and allowing body to sink into support of chair or floor. Release holding patterns by getting heavy. Feel your full density.

Tactile - Tracing fingertips along skin and various textures in environment. Engage nerve-rich hands as portals to present.

Tension areas - Scanning for areas of chronic tightness and warmth. Soften through exhales. Relax jaw, belly, neck, hips.

Interoception - Tuning into heart rate, digestion, hunger cues. How is body communicating its needs? Lovingly tending to these helps build autonomy and trust.

Body scans - Systematically sweeping attention through the body from toes to head, noting sensations without judgment.

Ecstatic dance - Letting body move and stretch intuitively to initiate blocked trauma energies coming back online.

By befriending the body's symphony of sensation, we guide awareness out of dissociation back into inhabiting our sensing flesh. Every body breathes with life waiting to be felt.

Reflections

- What science-based insights on mindfulness and meditation's benefits resonate most with your recovery journey?

- How has practicing mindfulness and meditation affected your capacity to regulate trauma responses and value your inner life?

- What mindfulness practices feel most accessible and helpful for you currently? Where do you still need to build skills?

Exercises

- Establish (or strengthen) a formal daily sitting meditation practice starting with just 5-10 minutes. Gradually increase over time. Observe the effects.

- Schedule mindfulness practices like conscious walking, mindful eating, sensing breath rhythms at various times throughout your day to build informal mindfulness habits.

- Make a self-soothing box with comforting items like photos, quotes, textured objects, scents, teas. Use it to practice being present when you feel highly distressed. Stay grounded in the now.

The present moment is always available to anchor us in wisdom if
we attune the senses. Keep returning to your breath, your footsteps,
the feeling of sunlight. This grounds trauma's chaos into calm.
You've got this.

Chapter 11: Fostering Post-Traumatic Growth and Resilience

Healing complex PTSD involves not just managing symptoms, but rising beyond to claim our full potential. We cultivate post-traumatic growth by drawing on inherent strengths to find meaning after trauma. Our reservations become our stepping stones. Suffering deepens purpose.

This chapter explores practices that foster resilience, empowerment, creativity, connection, and self-actualization. While the past left wounds, it also granted inner resources to harvest. We summon our warrior spirit to thrive, not just survive. Our phoenix rises from ashes.

Though recovery is challenging, you hold the pen to write the next chapter on your own terms, unbound by trauma's legacy. By releasing fear's hold, and awakening courage, extraordinary living awaits. The rest of your unfolding journey is yours to design.

Defining Resilience

Psychological resilience means effectively coping with adversity and adapting to life's inevitable challenges in healthy, constructive ways. It is the capacity to weather internal storms by tapping inner fortitude and wisdom.

Hallmarks of resilience include:

- Emotional flexibility navigating ups and downs without being derailed

- Actively problem-solving versus helplessly reacting when crisis hits

- Utilizing humor, creativity, and innovation to handle obstacles

- Cultivating networks of support during difficult times rather than isolating

- Deepening self-care practices that already build calm and focus

- Fostering post-traumatic growth by finding meaning in suffering

- Holding hope and perspective during periods of high distress

Resilience is not about avoiding pain, but learning to mindfully bear unavoidable hardship. We build the muscle memory that we can and will get through.

Neurobiology of Resilience

Modern brain research reveals resilience is a learnable skillset that alters neural pathways. Intentionally practicing supportive behaviors stimulates measurable brain changes.

Evidence-based ways to build resilient brain functioning include:

- **Stress inoculation** – Gradually increasing tolerance for adversities and discomforts through incremental exposure expands capacity. Taking small risks trains balance.

- **Optimism bias** – Forcefully countering negative thinking by actively identifying positive elements, outcomes, and contributions builds neural pathways for adaptive modeling of events. We see opportunity in obstacles.

- **Accelerated experiential dynamic psychotherapy (AEDP)** - This mindful self-healing therapy strengthens brain centers for self-regulation like the middle prefrontal cortex, allowing trauma survivors to intentionally calm reactive limbic and brainstem areas. New neural connections teach that arousal can be modulated.

- **Mindfulness meditation** – Multiple studies confirm regular meditation practice reduces trauma-related amygdala size while thickening prefrontal regions. Trauma survivors can thereby intentionally shift brain functioning from fear-based to higher order executive control.

- **Social support networks** – Our brains are wired for connection. Supportive relationships during adversity provide co-regulation of fear states that calms trauma conditioning and builds new neural pathways of safety and companionship.

We can rewire what trauma wired. Resilience flows from inner skills, not circumstantial fortune. With practice, we compose our mind as we wish.

Identifying Strengths

Healing complex trauma begins by cataloguing strengths and resources available to be mined. What tools, knowledge, past successes, role models, passions, and supports can we build on in the present journey? An inventory empowers.

Consider your:

- Personality strengths like humor, creativity, optimism, curiosity, bravery

- Principles and values providing moral compass when you are lost

- Interests, talents and skills mastered through practice

- Financial and material resources available

- Stories of overcoming past challenges that built confidence

- Cultural wisdom, rituals, and community support

- Access to nature and the insightful teachings it offers

- Model survivors who inspire possibility of healing

- Personal pharmacopeia of self-care tools that soothe and center

- Allies who genuinely care and offer perspective through dark times

You've already endured so much. Have compassion for all the ways you creatively adapted. Your reservoir of inner strengths runs deep, awaiting ultimate recovery.

Cultivating Optimism

Pervasive pessimism results from trauma's harsh lessons that the world is dangerous and unreliable. But optimism can be relearned by reframing stories about circumstances, other people's intentions, and possibilities. We release self-fulfilling prophecies based on past wounds.

Some ways to build optimism include:

Reality testing negative assumptions - Ask yourself "is this absolutely true or just my interpretation based on past experiences? What else could be positive here?" Make space for ambiguity.

Flexibility - Allow plans and expectations to change rather than cognitive rigidity. The future remains open to infinite possibilities. Stay out of mental ruts.

Opportunity seeking - Train yourself to naturally notice and point out possibilities in every circumstance for growth versus just anticipating downfalls.

Gratitude - Make regular time to appreciate present blessings. Savor moments of natural beauty, connection, progress, learning. Delight in small joys.

Self-compassion - Soften harsh inner voices fueling despair through talking to yourself as a caring friend would. You deserve this kindness.

Positive surroundings - Surround yourself with hopeful, kind people committed to goals larger than themselves. Limit time with negative influences.

Holistic health - Make self-care a priority. Sleep, nutrition, exercise, and play boost positive neurochemistry and perception.

Though cultivated gradually through practice, optimism liberates us to envision the full horizon of life again with curiosity and wonder.

Transforming Fear Into Excitement

Trauma breeds chronic fear and avoidance that constrain life. But the heightened arousal of fear serves almost identically to the arousal of excitement. By reframing our relationship to fear, we can transform it into fuel for engaging life.

Consider:

- Fear and excitement share racing heart, surging hormones, sweaty palms, and heightened attention indicating the brain cannot distinguish them.

- Avoidance provides temporary relief from fear but prevents learning fears are exaggerated. Lean toward anxiety and allow it to pass. Exposure builds resilience.

- Shift perspective - reframe the shaky knees and dry mouth that arise before public speaking, a date, or new challenge as excitement to tap into rather than dread. This transforms experience.

- Visualize feared situations ending positively, like giving an awkward speech and being met with applause or jelly legs before a rollercoaster that end in joy not danger. Write empowering endings.

- Recognize the physical sensation of fear as enthusiasm. Affirm to yourself, "I'm not anxious; I'm genuinely excited about this challenge!" Studies show that our choice of words can shape our perceptions.

- Share vulnerable stories of past courage with supportive others to build self-efficacy. Our feats seem greater reflected through other's eyes.

- When fears arise, affirm "I have survived this fear before, I can survive it again." Recall resources that enabled past perseverance.

We can retrain our brains to view challenges as exhilarating, not frightening. Boldness replaces avoidance. The world becomes our playground.

Core Values

Clarifying values provides compass bearings to guide choices when trauma's currents otherwise overwhelm. By repeatedly naming what matters most, priorities become lighthouses. We stop being pulled off course reactively.

Some reflection questions to identify core values:

- How do you want to experience relationships at their best? Love, safety, respect, care?

- What energizes and absorbs you? Creativity, music, ideas, connection, humor?

- What kind of impact do you want your life to have? Is it about justice, personal development, mending, helping others, or engaging in activism?

- What ethical principles govern your behavior such as respect, responsibility, integrity?

- What strengths and qualities in yourself and others do you most respect like courage, patience, vulnerability, determination?

- What replenishes you physically, mentally, emotionally, spiritually when depleted? Nature, beauty, affection, mindfulness, faith?

- What fears hold you back from living by your values like rejection, criticism, being duped? How could you move forward despite concerns?

- What excuses arise justifying value violations you need to release like "I was too busy, tired, stressed." Minimize defensiveness.

By naming our highest ideals, they light the path forward. Values structure growth through all things. What you want your journey to stand for will carry you through.

Setting Life Goals

Clarifying specific achievement aims channels energy productively versus stagnating in trauma reactions. Goals provide concrete embodiments of values. They sustain hope not just wishful thinking.

Some effective goal setting principles include:

Specificity - Describe each objective with exact and quantifiable criteria to make it evident when achieved. For example, compare "Release one article every month" with the more ambiguous "get writing out there.".

Timescales - Assign a specific completion date to create timeframe urgency versus indefinitely delaying. Break big goals into incremental milestones.

Small steps - Make initial goals bite-sized and achievable to build momentum versus getting overwhelmed by giant leaps. Consistent baby steps add up.

Positivity - Frame goals as additions you desire - new skills, experiences, contributions - rather than negatives to avoid which often backfire. Move toward passions.

Balance - Ensure goals reflect all life facets important to you like relationships, health, service, spirituality, creativity. Integrate your whole self.

Celebrate - Recognize each forward increment with care. Reward progress. Completion of every goal marks a tangible victory to savor.

Goals structure our striving with purpose and direction. They transform nebulous dreams into daily progress. Keep taking next steps. Destiny unfolds one foot in front of the other.

Anchoring in Five Senses

Trauma's grip manifests when locked in past-focused rumination versus fully engaging the present. But tuning into the body through the five senses quickly snaps us back into now. Sensory input overrides trauma's trance.

Try this grounding five senses practice:

1. **Sight** - Notice shapes, colors, textures. Study intricate details often missed. Allow beauty to restore perspective.

2. **Hearing** - Note ambient sounds near and far. Distinguish tones and locations. Listen without judging quality. Receive the soundscape.

3. **Smell** - Breathe in scents filling each space you inhabit. Savor subtler smells missed when rushing. Allow aromas to stir positive memories.

4. **Taste** - When eating, slow down to appreciate complex layers of flavors. Let their richness melt over tongue. Savor nourishing your body.

5. **Touch** - Run hands along various textured surfaces. Scout body for areas holding stress. Knead gently. Play with sand, clay, stones. Feel your way back into now.

Next time trauma's darkness calls, immerse yourself in sensory aliveness. Redirect focus each moment to the vibrancy of your breathing, tasting, smelling, touching, seeing body, here and now.

Skillful Action

Trauma often motivates distorted impulsive behavior attempts to hastily eradicate inner discomfort, rather than aligning action with values and intentions. Practicing mindful pause before reacting allows more skillful responses.

Try this 5 steps process:

1. **Inner signal** - When past trauma is activated, observe the related feelings, thoughts, and urges that emerge. Acknowledge them without self-criticism. For instance, say, "I'm experiencing anger and a desire to express it loudly."

2. **Pause** - Instead of reflexively reacting, pause to create space for choice. Take some deep breaths. Delay gives perspective.

3. **Question** - Ask yourself "Is this action actually serving me or just discharging pain temporarily? Will I regret it later? What behavior aligns better with my values?"

4. **Align** - After considering your thoughts, opt for a course of action that reflects your principles. You could choose to establish a non-confrontational boundary, create space to regain composure, or communicate your feelings honestly and considerately."

5. **Review** - After responding, congratulate mindful pauses. Note remaining trauma charge to continue processing. But appreciate successes disrupting patterns.

Each mindful pause interrupts ingrained reactivity. With care and repetition, trauma loses power to dictate thoughts, feelings, and actions. Your center leads.

Savoring Joy

Trauma and depression mute capacity for joy. But small daily practices that delight the senses, stir gratitude, soak in pleasure, and engage flow states reawaken and retrain neural pathways for easiness. Allow more sweetness.

Some ways to savor joy:

- Let music move you. Dance. Sing out loud.

- Savor favorite foods slowly. Appreciate nourishing your body.

- Stargaze. Lose yourself in the mysteries and vastness of the night sky.

- Spend time laughing, being silly, playing like a child.

- Light candles and incense. Infuse living space with gentle magic.

- Take relaxing baths with soothing music and clean pajamas waiting.

- Recall happy memories. Keep photo albums and journals of good times.

- Cuddle pets and take in their unconditional love.

- Express affection to loved ones often through hugs, kind words, and time together.

- Allow yourself to feel content and proud of progress made. You deserve this.

Though shadowed by adversity's weight, we gently re-ignite awareness of beauty surrounding us everywhere. Delight lives in exquisite ordinary moments we fail to notice when suffering preoccupies. Wake up to wonder. It heals.

Restorative Movement

Trauma leaves the body frozen and braced for danger. Gentle practices that relax muscular holding and encourage shaking, stretching, and embodiment move us out of collapse into freedom. We come home to the present vehicle that carries us.

Some forms of restorative movement:

TRE - Tension, Stress and Trauma Releasing Exercises involve consciously tremoring to discharge pent-up survival energy held in muscles.

Ecstatic dance - Freely dancing and moving the body intuitively to release inhibitions and trauma stored physically. Music guides.

Trauma-sensitive bodywork - Massage, acupuncture, Rolfing and other modalities combining touch with trauma education. Physical and emotional holding unravel together.

Walking meditation - Pausing frequently when walking to sense the body. Tight areas get invited to soften.

Authentic Movement - Spontaneously moving the body in ways intuitively guided from within versus choreographed.

Through gentle persistence, we awaken our animal selves that naturally shake off tension and inhabit each sensation. Our skin comes alive again.

Mindful Grounding

Sustaining consistent present-moment attention takes practice for trauma survivors accustomed to living reactively or on autopilot. But mindfulness builds gradually each time we catch our mind wandering and compassionately return focus.

Some ways to weave mindful grounding into daily life:

- When washing hands or dishes, tune into sensations - temperature, soap slippery texture. Fully arrive.

- Waiting in line, sense feet on floor, clothes touching skin, ambient sounds rather than getting impatient. Breathe.

- While eating, pause to feel textures in mouth, complex layers of taste, sensation of swallowing. Slow down.

- Walking outside, notice breeze on skin and colors appearing sharper with deep inhalations. Receive fully.

- In conversations, listen intently to words' meanings instead of just composing your response. Connect.

- Sit or lie down to scan entire body periodically, relaxing clenched areas through release breaths. Let gravity soften spine.

No moment stands alone. Begin threading mindfulness as an anchor cord through all activities. Over time, your lens widens to take in bare sensation behind stories.

Emotion Regulation Tools

Trauma survivors often still require external supports to counteract intense emotions until internal resources strengthen through recovery work. Using aids with compassion builds stability for staying present.

Some useful emotion regulation tools:

- **Exercise** - releases fight or flight hormones; elevates mood through endorphins

- **Journaling** - expresses overwhelming feelings safely on paper

- **Music** - regulates brainwave states and matches mood state

- **Nature walks** - disrupts rumination and calms nervous system

- **Cold water** - activates the diver's response to lower heart rate

- **Deep breathing** - activates the relaxation response via the vagus nerve

- **Talking with friends** - provides connection that reboots the system

- **Physical contact** - hugging offers mammalian reassurance through oxytocin

- **Creating art** - channels intense emotions into healthy outlets

- **Humor** - releases tension; provides perspective beyond painful feelings

Until inner stability strengthens, don't hesitate using healthy aids to stay grounded when overflowing. We all need assistance sometimes. You deserve support.

Reflections

- Looking back, what past challenges did you navigate more successfully than you realized at the time that built resilience?

- How could you channel heightened sensitivity and caretaking urges from complex trauma into empowering service, creativity or meaning?

- What inspires you most about the science and stories of post-traumatic growth emerging from darkness?

Exercises

- Make an inventory of internal strengths, knowledge, past wins, role models and supports. Revisit it whenever you doubt yourself during recovery.

- Think of a current obstacle. Brainstorm multiple perspectives, reframes, and solutions rather than just reflecting on what could go wrong. Build optimism.

- Write about a relationship rupture, disappointment or mistake. Explore self-compassion, lessons learned, forgiveness, making amends. Harvest growth.

You've got this. Keep growing and releasing past burdens through daily courage, care, and trust in your resilience. The life you most hope to live awaits your living. Keep healing.

Chapter 12: Living Fully in the Present

The culmination of healing complex PTSD involves releasing the past's grip to inhabit each moment with full passion and purpose. Staying radically present allows engagement versus ongoing trauma reactions. We stop living life through the veil of past wounds.

This final chapter explores practices for unhooking trauma's hold to stand firmly in today. By dropping dysfunctional coping, dropping limiting stories, and dropping resistance to what is, we feel alive for the very first time. We discover authentic freedom.

Though the path here is long, you have already come so far. Take heart. The next milestones await. Keep following trails to wide open vistas. Your most meaningful chapters lie ahead. You've got this. The view is worth it.

Assessing Safety

A pivotal milestone before releasing the past involves accurately evaluating current circumstances for objective safety so trauma responses don't persist reactively. We re-examine assumptions through a lens of compassion.

As you assess safety today, ask yourself:

- Are attachment relationships available now that provide consistent emotional attunement and care?

- What habits or situations continue exposing you to unnecessary risk or mistreatment?

- Do you possess more financial resources and stability now to meet your basic needs?

- Are there laws, policies and supports in place that were absent earlier and would have prevented past violations against you?

- What wider communities offer belonging and companionship if isolated previously?

- Do you have more knowledge, life experience and skills now to protect yourself if needed?

- What health behaviors help you care for your body with respect versus neglect?

- Can you identify empowering role models in addition to past hurtful ones?

While hypervigilance persists, notice where current circumstances truly differ from former traumatic ones. There are new tools to prevent repeating harm. An accurate assessment of present safety helps the brain update outdated programming.

Self-Efficacy

Trauma breeds a sense of helplessness and paralysis. But intentionally recalling past examples of resilience and courage builds confidence in our ability to productively handle challenges today. We overcome learned helplessness through expanded self-efficacy.

Consider times you have:

- Ended a detrimental relationship or departed from a harmful situation.

- Reported assault or abuse instead of remaining silent

- Face challenges without resorting to substances to numb the pain.

- Worked through conflict or misunderstandings directly

- Asked for help when overwhelmed instead of pretending to cope alone

- Learned an empowering new skill through consistent practice

- Forgave someone who harmed but changed for the better

- Mustered courage to speak your truth and be vulnerable

- Endured physical or emotional pain skillfully without being defined by it

- Rebounded from failures or disappointments and tried again

- Supported others unselfishly through their own darkness

- Let go resentment toward someone through understanding their past

Every experience of overcoming builds self-efficacy. Have compassion for all the ways you stayed strong. That courage remains within. You've got this.

Core Values

Clarifying values provides compass bearings to guide choices when trauma's currents otherwise overwhelm. By repeatedly naming what matters most, priorities become lighthouses. We stop being pulled off course reactively.

Some reflection questions to identify core values:

- How do you want to experience relationships at their best? Love, safety, respect, care?

- What energizes and absorbs you? Creativity, music, ideas, connection, humor?

- What kind of impact do you want your life to have? Is it about justice, personal development, mending, helping others, or engaging in activism?

- What ethical principles govern your behavior such as respect, responsibility, integrity?

- What strengths and qualities in yourself and others do you most respect like courage, patience, vulnerability, determination?

- What replenishes you physically, mentally, emotionally, spiritually when depleted? Nature, beauty, affection, mindfulness, faith?

- What fears hold you back from living by your values like rejection, criticism, being duped? How could you move forward despite concerns?

- What excuses arise justifying value violations you need to release like "I was too busy, tired, stressed." Minimize defensiveness.

By naming our highest ideals, they light the path forward. Values structure growth through all things. What you want your journey to stand for will carry you through.

Setting Life Goals

Clarifying specific achievement aims channels energy productively versus stagnating in trauma reactions. Goals provide concrete embodiments of values. They sustain hope not just wishful thinking.

Some effective goal setting principles include:

Specificity - Clearly outline each objective with specific and measurable criteria, making it evident when it's achieved. E.g. To publish one article per month

Timescales - Assign a specific completion date to create timeframe urgency versus indefinitely delaying. Break big goals into incremental milestones.

Small steps - Make initial goals bite-sized and achievable to build momentum versus getting overwhelmed by giant leaps. Consistent baby steps add up.

Positivity - Frame goals as additions you desire - new skills, experiences, contributions - rather than negatives to avoid which often backfire. Move toward passions.

Balance - Ensure goals reflect all life facets important to you like relationships, health, service, spirituality, creativity. Integrate your whole self.

Celebrate - Recognize each forward increment with care. Reward progress. Completion of every goal marks a tangible victory to savor.

Goals structure our striving with purpose and direction. They transform nebulous dreams into daily progress. Keep taking next steps. Destiny unfolds one foot in front of the other.

Anchoring in Five Senses

Trauma's grip manifests when locked in past-focused rumination versus fully engaging the present. But tuning into the body through the five senses quickly snaps us back into now. Sensory input overrides trauma's trance.

Try this grounding five senses practice:

1. **Sight** - Notice shapes, colors, textures. Study intricate details often missed. Allow beauty to restore perspective.

2. **Hearing** - Note ambient sounds near and far. Distinguish tones and locations. Listen without judging quality. Receive the soundscape.

3. **Smell** - Breathe in scents filling each space you inhabit. Savor subtler smells missed when rushing. Allow aromas to stir positive memories.

4. **Taste** - When eating, slow down to appreciate complex layers of flavors. Let their richness melt over tongue. Savor nourishing your body.

5. **Touch** - Run hands along various textured surfaces. Scout body for areas holding stress. Knead gently. Play with sand, clay, stones. Feel your way back into now.

Next time trauma's darkness calls, immerse yourself in sensory aliveness. Redirect focus each moment to the vibrancy of your breathing, tasting, smelling, touching, seeing body, here and now.

Skillful Action

Trauma often motivates distorted impulsive behavior attempts to hastily eradicate inner discomfort, rather than aligning action with values and intentions. Practicing mindful pause before reacting allows more skillful responses.

Try this 5 step process:

1. **Internal alert** - When trauma is activated, observe the sensations, thoughts, and urges that come with it. Identify them without directing blame towards yourself. For instance, recognize "I am feeling anger and an inclination to express it loudly."

2. **Pause** - Instead of reflexively reacting, pause to create space for choice. Take some deep breaths. Delay gives perspective.

3. **Question** - Ask yourself "Is this action actually serving me or just discharging pain temporarily? Will I regret it later? What behavior aligns better with my values?"

4. **Align** - After considering your thoughts, opt for a course of action that reflects your principles. You could choose to establish a non-confrontational boundary, create space to regain composure, or communicate your feelings honestly and considerately."

5. **Review** - After responding, congratulate mindful pauses. Note remaining trauma charge to continue

processing. But appreciate successes disrupting patterns.

Each mindful pause interrupts ingrained reactivity. With care and repetition, trauma loses power to dictate thoughts, feelings, and actions. Your center leads.

Savoring Joy

Trauma and depression mute capacity for joy. But small daily practices that delight the senses, stir gratitude, soak in pleasure, and engage flow states reawaken and retrain neural pathways for easiness. Allow more sweetness.

Some ways to savor joy:

- Let music move you. Dance. Sing out loud.

- Savor favorite foods slowly. Appreciate nourishing your body.

- Stargaze. Lose yourself in the mysteries and vastness of the night sky.

- Spend time laughing, being silly, playing like a child.

- Light candles and incense. Infuse living space with gentle magic.

- Take relaxing baths with soothing music and clean pajamas waiting.

- Recall happy memories. Keep photo albums and journals of good times.

- Cuddle pets and take in their unconditional love.

- Express affection to loved ones often through hugs, kind words, and time together.

- Allow yourself to feel content and proud of progress made. You deserve this.

Though shadowed by adversity's weight, we gently re-ignite awareness of beauty surrounding us everywhere. Delight lives in exquisite ordinary moments we fail to notice when suffering preoccupies. Wake up to wonder. It heals.

Restorative Movement

Trauma leaves the body frozen and braced for danger. Gentle practices that relax muscular holding and encourage shaking, stretching, and embodiment move us out of collapse into freedom. We come home to the present vehicle that carries us.

Some forms of restorative movement:

TRE - Tension, Stress and Trauma Releasing Exercises involve consciously tremoring to discharge pent-up survival energy held in muscles.

Ecstatic dance - Freely dancing and moving the body intuitively to release inhibitions and trauma stored physically. Music guides.

Trauma-sensitive bodywork - Massage, acupuncture, Rolfing and other modalities combining touch with trauma education. Physical and emotional holding unravel together.

Walking meditation - Pausing frequently when walking to sense the body. Tight areas get invited to soften.

Authentic Movement - Spontaneously moving the body in ways intuitively guided from within versus choreographed.

Through gentle persistence, we awaken our animal selves that naturally shake off tension and inhabit each sensation. Our skin comes alive again.

Mindful Grounding

Sustaining consistent present-moment attention takes practice for trauma survivors accustomed to living reactively or on autopilot. But mindfulness builds gradually each time we catch our mind wandering and compassionately return focus.

Some ways to weave mindful grounding into daily life:

- When washing hands or dishes, tune into sensations - temperature, soap slippery texture. Fully arrive.

- Waiting in line, sense feet on floor, clothes touching skin, ambient sounds rather than getting impatient. Breathe.

- While eating, pause to feel textures in mouth, complex layers of taste, sensation of swallowing. Slow down.

- Walking outside, notice breeze on skin and colors appearing sharper with deep inhalations. Receive fully.

- In conversations, listen intently to words' meanings instead of just composing your response. Connect.

- Sit or lie down to scan entire body periodically, relaxing clenched areas through release breaths. Let gravity soften spine.

No moment stands alone. Begin threading mindfulness as an anchor cord through all activities. Over time, your lens widens to take in bare sensation behind stories.

Emotion Regulation Tools

Trauma survivors often still require external supports to counteract intense emotions until internal resources strengthen through recovery work. Using aids with compassion builds stability for staying present.

Some useful emotion regulation tools:

- **Exercise** - releases fight or flight hormones; elevates mood through endorphins

- **Journaling** - expresses overwhelming feelings safely on paper

- **Music** - regulates brainwave states and matches mood state

- **Meditation** - returns focus to the present moment

- **Nature walks** - disrupts rumination and calms nervous system

- **Cold water** - activates the diver's response to lower heart rate

- **Deep breathing** - activates the relaxation response via the vagus nerve

- **Talking with friends** - provides connection that reboots the system

- **Physical contact** - hugging offers mammalian reassurance through oxytocin

- **Creating art** - channels intense emotions into healthy outlets

- **Humor** - releases tension; provides perspective beyond painful feelings

Until inner stability strengthens, don't hesitate using healthy aids to stay grounded when overflowing. We all need assistance sometimes. You deserve support.

Evaluating Relationships

Taking inventory of current relationships becomes essential to determine which support healing versus maintain dysfunction. Instead of traumatic bonds, choose bonds fostering trust, respect, care and gradual opening.

Qualities to assess in relationships:

- Safe - Do I feel physically and emotionally secure? Can I be appropriately vulnerable?

- Attuned - Is the other sincerely interested in knowing and responding helpfully to my needs?

- Available - Does the other prioritize our connection and show up reliably?

- Boundaried - Can I voice preferences without manipulation or punishment? Are separateness and privacy respected?

- Communicative - Do interactions involve open listening, speaking truth with care, and collaborative conflict resolution?

- Consistent - Is the other stable and predictable in mood, follow-through, and commitment to me?

- Self-responsible - Does the other handle their own emotions and past without blaming me? Are they accountable for how their actions affect me?

Healthy relating fosters expansion versus chaos, paralysis, or shrinking. Fill life with those who help you grow into your fullest self. Prune the rest.

Skill of No

Trauma leaves survivors prone to compliance and poor boundaries. But politely saying "no" builds essential autonomy, self-trust, and consent rather than passively accepting anything coercive or depleting. Start small.

Ways to practice saying no:

- Decline non-essential invites by politely responding "I can't make it but thanks for the invite!" No excuses needed.

- When asked for favors that over-extend you, say "I'm not able to help with that right now, but wish you the best."

- With those who take advantage frequently, reply "I can't continue to give that, but I hope you find support." Broken records persist.

- To those pressuring you into unwanted activities, say firmly "That doesn't work for me, but I'm sure you'll find others interested." Hold your ground.

- "When faced with disrespect, insist that it ceases by expressing, 'I am not comfortable with this. Please treat me with respect.' Establish clear boundaries.

- If others project unreal expectations, clarify "I can't take that on for you." You decide how much feels right.

- To unwanted touch, loudly say "Please do not touch me without my consent!"

Keep politely declining anything that forces, drains, or violates you. Your needs and consent matter. Take back power by simply yet firmly saying no.

Self-Nurturing Skills

Healing complex trauma requires reparenting ourselves with the unconditional care early neglect denied. Start small. Each act of basic self-care builds trust in your right to nurture and intrinsic worth.

Some simple self-nurturing practices:

- Prepare nourishing meals and eat slowly with gratitude

- Wrap yourself in blankets when needing containment

- Verbally comfort emotions through saying "I'm here for you. This will pass."

- Light candles, take bubble baths, do your hair to feel cared for

- Treat yourself occasionally to massages, nature walks, favorite foods

- Keep living space clean, tidy and beautiful

- Speak gently to yourself as you would a child – with patience, care, reassurance

- Maintain regular sleep routines to ensure rest

- Buy yourself small gifts just because - flowers, art supplies, jewelry

- Express understanding when you fail or emotions overwhelm. Forgive mistakes.

- Make time for play, creativity, laughter, lightness

Parent yourself back to wholeness through meeting your own needs consistently. You deserve nurturance. Keep planting seeds of self-care until they bloom.

Inner Child Work

Recovering involves reparenting wounded parts still holding trauma through providing the subconscious nurturance missed in childhood. We rebuild secure attachment internally.

Some ways to approach inner child work:

- Close your eyes and picture yourself as a child when trauma occurred. Witness through adult eyes their pain, confusion, and unmet needs.

- Dialogue with your inner child. Share your insights and perspectives from adult consciousness to bring new understanding about events to their frozen-in-time beliefs.

- Channel unconditional love and safety to the child within. Comfort their hurts through words, visualization, and gentle touch like softly stroking your arm. Defend them from destructive messages that misshaped their identity.

- Grieve what your inner child endured and still carries in pain. Express outrage for the unjust violations enacted upon their innocence. Protect and cherish them.

- Appreciate the creative survival strategies of your inner child that kept you alive. Their weaknesses were actually strengths in context. Honor their resilience and tenacity.

- Tell your inner child about positives in your life now they could not have envisioned. Share that they grew up and have many choices.

- Create spaces for your inner child to play, be silly, express creativity, feel cared for. Fulfill their unmet developmental needs.

Through compassionately reparenting internal fragmented parts, we integrate dissociated memories into present consciousness. The past rests while we vibrantly inhabit today, nurturing ourselves fully at last.

Life Purpose

Clarifying passionate aims and declaring core pursuits calms trauma's chaos by orienting our days with meaning. Purpose channels trauma's heightened energy in empowering directions. Define what you stand for.

Some ways to identify life purpose:

- What pulls at your heart? What breaks your heart? What do you ache to change or contribute?

- When do you experience the most vitality and complete absorption? When does the concept of time seem to vanish?

- Look back on key turning points. When did you feel guided or that "still small voice"?

- What are your natural talents and strengths? What skills do you want to cultivate and offer?

- What values feel non-negotiable to you? What matters most at the end of life?

- If you had unlimited resources/health/time, what would you dedicate yourself to?

- What principles do you aim to embody in your life? How would you prefer to be recalled or remembered?

- Imagine you are 90 years old giving advice to your current self. What wisdom emerges?

By declaring purpose, we claim our lives rather than remain passive. Our pain transforms into meaning. Each day orients around what we stand for.

Reflections

- How have you noticed your relationship to past trauma and symptoms evolving in ways that allow fuller engagement in each present moment?

- What recovery practices and insights have been most pivotal in building capacity to live more fully despite shadows of past trauma?

- Reflect on moments recently you felt most in tune with senses aliveness, purpose, inner wisdom, and freedom from the past's grip. What facilitated this?

Exercises

- Pick an upcoming event you feel worried about. Write out best, moderate, and worst-case scenarios. Then make a plan of accepted action for each. Practice tolerating uncertainty.

- Do an audit of how you spend your time each day last week. Does it align with your core values? Make needed adjustments.

- Pick a new perspective or belief to strengthen like self-compassion. Make a 30 day challenge practicing thoughts and behaviors that fortify it. Create neural pathways for positive change.

You've got this. Keep growing and releasing past burdens through daily courage, care, and trust in your resilience. The life you most hope to live awaits your living. Keep healing.

Conclusion: Your Recovery Journey

If you are reading these words, congratulations. You have come far already on the courageous road of healing from complex developmental trauma. By educating yourself on CPTSD and undertaking your own recovery process, you are claiming your power and testimony.

This book traces a path from understanding complex trauma's origins and common impacts through tangible skills for processing painful memories, transforming unhealthy relational patterns, and releasing the past's grip to live fully. We end by arriving home in ourselves - embracing our corresponding darkness and light.

However, there isn't a single book that holds all the answers. Your personal experiences and truths hold greater importance than any professional structure. Embrace what resonates with you from here and discard what doesn't. There are countless paths toward healing, and you get to trust and follow the way that calls uniquely to your spirit. You remain the expert on your inner wisdom.

If the journey ahead feels daunting, take heart remembering all you have already survived and overcome through sheer determination and resilience. Those same strengths that enabled you to endure adversity equip you now to transform and transcend it. Have compassion for all you carry as fellow travelers - your creativity, sensitivity, fierce loyalty and boundless love that shined despite everything. You are a living miracle. Keep re-reading that last sentence as needed!

While complex PTSD often compounds challenges through its impacts on self-worth, emotion regulation, relationships and functioning, it has no power to destroy your core essence, values, talents, and humanity. Symptoms reflect adaptations, not personal flaws or deficiencies. Breathe this truth in daily. You are and always were inherently whole, good, worthy of nurturance, belonging, and joy. Trauma alone does not define you.

Yet the wounds of complex trauma also undeniably cut deep through the psyche and physiology. Recognize all the ways adversity understandably conditioned your perceptions, behaviors, and nervous system responses. Of course, pervasive violation, deprivation, or chaos during key developmental phases affects how we subconsciously operate in relationships and the larger world through adaptive survival strategies learned young. This does not signify damage, only profound hurt desperately needing tending through patient compassion - both inwardly and through safe therapeutic relationships.

As you walk this winding path of recovery, proceed first with gentleness. Allow time to grieve painful pasts while learning to ground yourself ever more fully in the present moment, here and now, where you are absolutely safe and life awaits unfolding however you wish. You get to write the remaining chapters. After trauma's detour, how will you script the next leg of your unique heroic journey?

Of course the work of processing traumatic memories and addressing attachment wounds remains vital, yet need not re-traumatize when approached gradually, at your own pace, with ample inner and external resourcing. This material asks to be integrated so you can live more fully rather than expending energy suppressing it. With courage and support, we slowly digest that which could not be digested at the time. In fits and starts, confusion yields to coherence. We reconstruct empowering self-narratives that redeem the past and feed the future.

As symptoms like flashbacks, emotional volatility, negative self-talk, and relationship chaos recede through acquiring new skills, you will uncover lost parts of self waiting to be claimed. Your grounded, discerning, confident, curious, joyful core self awaits behind those protective adaptations. Integrate any split-off inner identities back into the wholeness of your being. Playfulness, creativity, fascination, and inspiration get freed up when not constantly hypervigilant. There is so much yet to experience and express. Your soul wants dancing again.

Of course be prepared for the messy nonlinearity of recovery. Ups and downs are inevitable along this ride. Breakthroughs and major setbacks will alternate. When periods of regression occur, respond to yourself and your healing with even deeper compassion, care, and commitment. Talk to yourself as you would a beloved friend, reminding "you've got this, this too shall pass." Our systems seem to grow the most following decompensation. Have faith in larger forces supporting your expansion.

Progress transcending complex developmental trauma requires patience - both active fortitude and passive allowing. Rush nothing. But also do not stall. Meet each inner step and backslide with courageous investigation versus judgement. Keep growing your self-knowledge. From breakdowns, breakthroughs get born. You will come to trust your inner capacity to navigate storms. At times the light goes out, but only so it may be reignited brighter. You will find your way.

While formal psychotherapy, somatic therapies, support groups, medication, and complementary modalities often prove invaluable formats on the healing path, do not underestimate the power of daily informal practices to unravel trauma's stuck energies and narratives. Simple rituals give structure for transformation. The light touch sometimes dislodges deepest hold.

Actively care for your body through soothing nutrition, sleep, movement, and touch. Immerse often in nature's intricacies. Express through journaling, art, music, poetry. Allow play and childlike wonder to return. Set firm boundaries and practice saying no. Take incremental risks trying new activities that pique curiosity. Share vulnerably with safe others. Catalog inner strengths and past victories. Clarify core values. Delight in overlooked beauty surrounding you right now.

Keep up mindfulness, meditation, breathing practices. Stay tenderly anchored in your senses, grounded in the present. When trauma gets triggered, respond with care not self-attack. You deserve compassion, patience and comfort. Slowly over time, with belief in your own resilience, one day you will realize you have not thought about the past in weeks because your mind rests immersed in the aliveness of now.

This expanded capacity for fully engaging each moment - for feeling at home peaceful in your body and savoring sensory pleasures - liberates your destiny going forward. You get to stop surviving and start thriving. You reclaim freedom to create, explore, connect, serve, and cherish existence as you see fit, unbound by the weight of trauma.

When you no longer hand over power by remaining chained to the past, your reborn vitality chooses wisely how to spend your remaining days. Some questions to reflect on periodically to stay aligned with your evolving purpose and priorities:

- How do I wish to feel when I wake up each morning - calm, vibrant, grateful? What morning routines support this? What energizes me?

- How do I hope to move through each day - engaged, serene, friendly, helpful? What activities and interactions feed my spirit?

- How do I want to feel as I prepare for bed each night - content, peaceful, appreciated? What evening rituals would nurture this? How do I wish to be in relationship with myself?

- If today were my last chance to inhabit this wondrous body on this miraculous planet, how would I spend it? Who would I connect with? What words would I wish to impart?

- When I envision reaching the end of my life looking back, what memories most bring me joy? How will I have contributed using my gifts? Who will I have loved? What moments will feel precious?

Orient each day around drawing these future memories into being whether through creative expression, activism, learning, connection, or slowing down to fully taste this passing grace of being. What fulfills your wild and precious soul? Your presence is a gift; be intentional in sharing it.

There will always be forces of fear, separation, blind consumption, and lesser impulses pulling us from our birthright vitality. But once we reconnect to the sacred wholeness within, we can respond to these destructive forces with compassion while standing firm in self-honoring purpose. We stop fighting trauma's power externally to instead live aligned with cherished values from the inside-out. We inhabit our unshakeable belonging.

Of course there will also be loss, grief, and injustice that weigh heavy even the most well-tended psyche. Let your enlarged capacity hold space for the necessary tears. But recall always that darkness prepares the soil for coming light. Difficult seasons bear beauty if we tend patiently with faith in their necessity. You belong here, blooming exquisitely, even through shadows. Release fear's grip. The only way out is through.

Much lay in ruin once, but see how new growth has found footing regardless. One gentle lesson learned from trauma's devastation is that hope persists beyond all ration. Love still finds a way through clearest cracks. And when the severing hour reveals more sky than anticipated, we remember life never withheld itself at all. It only waited for our arriving.

So take heart. Have courage. And keep going. Your soul - so much larger than trauma, so anchored in eternal truth - already recognizes the way through winding uncertainty. Align each step with purpose and community. Protect your tender shoots. Receive the grace prepared since time's conception to flood perfectly your path, illuminating direction home. You've got this.

On this journey, your life becomes the prayer and the answer. And you get to write the prayer anew each day, naming the destiny that calls uniquely through your voice and your voice alone. Yours is a story still unfolding that none will ever live just as you will. Be bold in authoring its next redemptive arc.

The work of a lifetime awaits full of meaning. Beyond struggle, your expanded heart beats. Listen to its wisdom. Stay the course. Even darkness births stars. Beginning now, allow joy and healing. The light you seek resides already within you, ready to bloom courageously once nourished by self-care, community, and trust in your innate goodness and belonging. Keep following unseen forces pulling you home from the inside-out.

May you feel loved, safe, hopeful. May you live with purpose and passion. May you know peace.

Keep going. You've got this. The view ahead is so very beautiful, and you deserve to see it. We're glad you're here.

Appendix A: Worksheets and Exercises

This appendix compiles helpful worksheets, reflections, and exercises from each chapter into one convenient place to support your recovery journey. Feel free to photocopy and use any pages that resonate.

Chapter 1 - Symptoms and Impacts

Chapter Reflections:

- What complex PTSD symptoms do you identify with most right now? When did you first notice them arise?

- How have these symptoms adapted you for survival in the past? Reflect with self-compassion.

- What impact do your complex trauma symptoms have on different life domains today? What would you like to see change?

Chapter Exercises:

- Make a timeline of when you first noticed different complex PTSD symptoms emerge. What experiences may have contributed to each one?

- Write a letter to yourself expressing understanding and care for the complex PTSD symptoms you currently struggle with. Affirm strengths and capacities that enabled you to survive.

- Make a list of the top 5 strategies that help you feel better when symptoms are intensified. Keep it handy for when destabilized.

Chapter 2 - Causes and Risk Factors

Chapter Reflections:

- How do your own childhood experiences relate to causes of complex trauma described in this chapter? What formative events do you associate with the onset of symptoms?

- Without judgment, identify any risk factors or developmental vulnerabilities that may have affected your childhood. How could you have been better supported?

- Take a moment to remember you were never to blame for childhood trauma, no matter the circumstances. Affirm your inherent worth.

Chapter Exercises:

- Write a letter of understanding and compassion to your younger self about the origins of your complex trauma. Affirm the strengths that enabled you to survive.

- Draw a timeline of key events and periods in your childhood, both positive and traumatic. Identify developmental stages impacted and emerging symptoms.

- Make a list of nurturing words and comforting actions your inner child still needs to hear and feel now. Identify caring people in your life today who can provide this.

Chapter 3 - The Neuroscience of Trauma

- How does understanding trauma's impact on the brain affect your self-perception and self-compassion?

- Which neurobiological effects of early adversity resonate most with your current challenges and symptoms?

- What encouragement arises knowing your brain retains lifelong capacity for change through new learning?

Chapter Exercises:

- Research how secure attachment experiences rewire neural pathways. Identify potential sources of corrective bonding for you today.

- Make a list of daily practices that could build the new neural circuitry you aspire to: meditation, art, affirmations, etc. Schedule time to engage.

- Notice everyday moments when you shift from fear-based neural firing to peace or empowerment. Write them down.

Chapter 4 - Establishing Safety, Stability and Self-Care

Chapter Reflections:

- What self-care elements feel most essential for you in stabilizing early recovery? Which most need strengthening?

- How could establishing consistent daily routines help provide needed structure? Identify 1-2 you will try implementing.

- Where do you feel safest right now - internally, relationally, environmentally? What needs improvement?

Chapter Exercises:

- Make lists of triggers, grounding skills, and self-soothing tools. Keep them handy when destabilized. Revisit and update regularly.

- Write about a time you successfully endured intense emotions or flashbacks. Identify the skills and inner strengths you drew upon. Reaffirm your capacity to handle adversity.

- Create a detailed self-care plan addressing nutrition, sleep, movement, social support, nature time, and routines. Refer to it daily. Revise as needed.

Chapter 5 - Processing Traumatic Memories

Chapter Reflections:

- What past traumatic memories feel most important for you to process in pursuing healing? How do you feel about approaching this?

- What forms of therapy or self-guided practices resonate for unpacking and integrating these old hurts?

- How have you noticed traumatic memories losing their intensity and grip on you as you've started processing them?

Chapter Exercises:

- Journal about a traumatic childhood memory, exploring associated images, emotions, body sensations, storyline, meanings made. Notice if its charge lessens through writing.

- Make a playlist of songs that provide comfort, empowerment, and compassion. Listen when memories of past traumas arise to help digest them.

- Draw or paint whatever arises as you reflect on a particular traumatic memory. Express through color, shapes, symbols. No need to judge creative process.

Chapter 6 - Transforming Your Relationship to Trauma

Chapter Reflections:

- How has your relationship to past trauma evolved through the recovery process so far?

- What key shifts in awareness and perspective have allowed you to separate it from your present identity and worth?

- What metaphors or meanings around your trauma story bring you comfort and direction?

- How has trauma shaped your values, interests, skills, and sources of meaning without solely defining you?

- What practices or therapeutic approaches have been most helpful for transforming your trauma responses?

- What feels needed to keep deepening your healing journey toward thriving?

Chapter Exercises:

- Draw or write about your trauma like it was a weather pattern – a storm that passed through but did not remain. How is the forecast different now?

- List empowering affirmative statements about your core self, beneath the trauma story, that affirm your strengths, worth, and humanity.

- Draw or write a letter to your inner child parts explaining your adult perspectives on past events and offering them new nurturance.

- Create art, music, or poetry that symbolizes your process of recovering from past trauma. Let it depict transformation.

- Design a personal ritual to honor your emergence into a new phase of recovery. Enact it in some way.

- If it feels safe, share parts of your recovery story with someone supportive. Break secrecy that gives trauma power. Receive grace.

Chapter 7 - Managing Emotional Flashbacks and Triggers

Chapter Reflections:

- What passive and active coping strategies help you most in surviving flashbacks when they arise?

- How have you strengthened capacity to navigate triggering situations with more consciousness and skill over time?

- What science-based insights and skills from this chapter could you apply to defuse flashbacks and triggers?

Chapter Exercises:

- Make a log tracking flashbacks - dates, triggers, associated emotions, thoughts, physical sensations. Look for patterns over time.

- Design a detailed safety plan for when flashbacks become overwhelming - grounding practices, supports to activate, ways to show self-compassion.

- Practice noticing precursor warning signs like muscle tension that signal you're triggered. Take heart each time you catch activation early before escalating.

Chapter 8 - Building Healthy Relationships and Attachment

Chapter Reflections:

- What new relational skills and practices outlined in this chapter resonate most with your growth edges in recovery? Where do you want to build capacity?

- Reflect on moments recently you handled relationships in healthier more conscious ways than you may have in the past before recovery. Appreciate evidence of progress.

- Consider ways spirituality or commitment to values larger than the self could help stabilize and soothe you when interpersonal ruptures occur.

- What inner work around attachment wounds still feels needed? What internalized templates or narratives ask for updating?

Chapter Exercises:

- Make a two column list exploring your current relationships - which feel healing vs. draining/toxic. Consider ways to invest more in the life-giving bonds.

- Practice expressing vulnerable emotions or asking directly for support in relationships where it feels safe. Build trust in risking connection after past violations.

- Journal a letter speaking your truth compassionately to someone you struggle relating to due to past hurt. What could heal this bond? What inner work remains?

Chapter 9 - Rediscovering Purpose and Meaning

Chapter Reflections:

- What activities and pursuits feel most meaningful, energizing and absorbing for you? How could you allocate more time to these?

- How could turning wounds into service for others help transform past pain into healing impact?

- What dreams and passions suppressed in the past feel important to revive and integrate? What first steps could you take?

Chapter Exercises:

- Write about an adversity or violation from your past. Explore metaphoric meanings, life lessons, reflections on human nature. Harvest wisdom.

- Make a bucket list of desired future activities, creative projects, adventures, acts of service. Schedule regular reflection on which to take tangible action steps toward.

- Draw or collage your ideal future life incorporating purpose, community, self-care, nature, fun. Make it vibrant and inspiring. Place it where you see it often.

Chapter 10 - Practicing Mindfulness and Emotional Regulation

Chapter Reflections:

- What science-based insights on mindfulness and meditation's benefits resonate most with your recovery journey?

- How has practicing mindfulness and meditation affected your capacity to regulate trauma responses and value your inner life?

- What mindfulness practices feel most accessible and helpful for you currently? Where do you still need to build skills?

Chapter Exercises:

- Establish (or strengthen) a formal daily sitting meditation practice starting with just 5-10 minutes. Gradually increase over time. Observe the effects.

- Schedule mindfulness practices like conscious walking, mindful eating, sensing breath rhythms at various times throughout your day to build informal mindfulness habits.

- Make a self-soothing box with comforting items like photos, quotes, textured objects, scents, teas. Use it to practice being present when you feel highly distressed. Stay grounded in the now.

Chapter 11 - Fostering Post-Traumatic Growth and Resilience

Chapter Reflections:

- Looking back, what past challenges did you navigate more successfully than you realized at the time that built resilience?

- How could you channel heightened sensitivity and caretaking urges from complex trauma into empowering service, creativity or meaning?

- What inspires you most about the science and stories of post-traumatic growth emerging from darkness?

Chapter Exercises:

- Make an inventory of internal strengths, knowledge, past wins, role models and supports. Revisit it whenever you doubt yourself during recovery.

- Think of a current obstacle. Brainstorm multiple perspectives, reframes, and solutions rather than just reflecting on what could go wrong. Build optimism.

- Write about a relationship rupture, disappointment or mistake. Explore self-compassion, lessons learned, forgiveness, making amends. Harvest growth.

Chapter 12 - Living Fully in the Present

Chapter Reflections:

- How have you noticed your relationship to past trauma and symptoms evolving in ways that allow fuller engagement in each present moment?

- What recovery practices and insights have been most pivotal in building capacity to live more fully despite shadows of past trauma?

- Reflect on moments recently you felt most in tune with senses aliveness, purpose, inner wisdom, and freedom from the past's grip. What facilitated this?

Chapter Exercises:

- Pick an upcoming event you feel worried about. Write out best, moderate, and worst case scenarios. Then make a plan of accepted for each. Practice tolerating uncertainty.

- Do an audit of how you spend your time each day last week. Does it align with your core values? Make needed adjustments.

- Pick a new perspective or belief to strengthen like self-compassion. Make a 30 day challenge practicing thoughts and behaviors that fortify it. Create neural pathways for positive change.

You've got this. Keep growing and releasing past burdens through daily courage, care, and trust in your resilience. The life you most hope to live awaits your living. Keep healing.

Appendix B: Resources for Recovery

This appendix provides a list of books, workbooks, websites, and other helpful resources to support your healing journey with complex PTSD.

Books

The Body Keeps the Score: Brain, Mind, and Body in the Healing of Trauma by Bessel van der Kolk - Bestseller explores the biology and psychology of trauma's impacts. Discusses innovative treatment approaches.

Complex PTSD: From Surviving to Thriving by Pete Walker - Highly recommended guide explaining complex PTSD and symptoms. Outlines actionable coping tools and recovery concepts.

The PTSD Workbook by Mary Beth Williams and Soili Poijula - Practical exercises and education to manage trauma symptoms, build resilience, and create meaning.

Healing Developmental Trauma by Laurence Heller and Aline LaPierre - Compassionate guide using somatic experiencing approach to releasing trauma stored in the body and nervous system.

The Emotionally Absent Mother by Jasmin Lee Cori - Examines the impacts of emotionally unavailable, selfish, or narcissistic mothering figures. Discusses healing attachment wounds.

The Tao of Fully Feeling by Pete Walker – Using mindfulness, this book offers detailed guidance for identifying and finding balance in difficult emotions.

Healing Sexual Violence by Staci Haines – Provides survivor stories, somatic practices, and careful guidance to support healing from sexual trauma specifically.

The Body Remembers Volume 2 by Babette Rothschild – Explains trauma's physiological effects and body-based therapy approaches to restore regulation abilities.

Workbooks

The PTSD Workbook for Teens by Libbi Palmer - User-friendly exercises to understand trauma's impacts, build coping skills, and cultivate self-compassion in aftermath of complex trauma.

The Complex PTSD Workbook by Arielle Schwartz - Structured exercises using goal setting, coping skills, and meaning making to understand and overcome complex PTSD.

Healing Exercises and Education for Abused Adults by Bonnie Burstow - Practical skills drawn from a range of therapies for managing emotions, thinking patterns, relationships and trauma memory processing.

The Dialectical Behavior Therapy Skills Workbook by Matthew McKay - Builds emotion regulation, distress tolerance, mindfulness and interpersonal skills via structured worksheets.

The Cognitive Behavioral Coping Skills Workbook for PTSD by Matthew Tull - Uses CBT approaches to address unhelpful thinking patterns, build coping strategies, and develop healthy new behaviors after trauma.

Websites

OutoftheStorm.website – Pete Walker's in-depth blog exploring complex trauma with a range of articles and insights to aid recovery.

BeautyAfterBruises.org - Nonprofit focused on complex PTSD recovery through education, skills building and survivor stories. Offers online support groups.

ChildhoodPTSD.org - Provides education on developmental trauma and complex PTSD. Includes mood journal, meditation recordings, blog posts by trauma professionals supporting healing.

ComplexPTSD.net - Informational site on the science, symptoms and treatment approaches for complex PTSD. Includes personal essays by trauma survivors.

TidyingUpTrauma.com – Blog exploring the intersection of healing complex trauma, professional organizing, and mindfulness. Many relatable personal essays.

SomaticExperiencing.org – Explains trauma's physiological impacts and somatic therapy approaches to processing and releasing stored traumatic energies in the body and nervous system.

Support Groups

AdultChildren.org - 12-step recovery program for adults raised in alcoholic or otherwise dysfunctional homes. Local in-person and online meetings available.

Sidran.org - Nonprofit with local in-person and online support groups for trauma survivors and loved ones. Some groups specific for PTSD, dissociation, childhood abuse, etc.

Meetup.com - Search this site for in-person groups related to trauma recovery, PTSD, empowerment, mindfulness and complementary holistic approaches. Filter by location.

AfterSilence.org - Active online forums to share stories and support healing for trauma and PTSD related to sexual violence specifically. Moderated for safety.

PsychologyToday.com - Find therapists, psychiatrists, support groups and treatment centers. Searchable database lists provider profiles, specialties and insurance accepted.

Apps

PTSD Coach - Free app from National Center for PTSD providing education about symptoms, self-assessment, coping tools, crisis resources. For both veterans and civilian trauma.

CPTSD: Help & Healing - Relaxation and mindfulness meditations created specifically for complex PTSD. Additional educational articles.

Calm - Popular app with wide range of meditation, sleep stories, breathing program and movement videos for mindfulness, stress reduction and sleep.

What's Up? - CBT based app teaching coping skills for anxiety, panic, depression, and PTSD through assessments, tools, quotes, and peer support forum.

InsightTimer - Free meditation app with thousands of guided practices, music tracks, groups and classes specializing in healing trauma.

breathwrk - Short guided breathing exercises focused specifically on using the breath to reduce anxiety, manage cravings, improve sleep, and lower stress.

SuperBetter - Game-based app to cultivate optimism, strength-finding, and resilience when dealing with health challenges using small achievable quests. Fun weekly activities.

Youper - AI chatbot for CBT techniques to manage difficult emotions, negative self-talk, unhealthy habits. Check in daily, set goals, track progress over weeks.

Sources of Strength - Evidence based app and program cultivating hope, help and strength in yourself and peers. Uplifting messages and simple actions. Great for teens.

Podcasts

Complextrauma Podcast - Interviews trauma specialists like Bessel van der Kolk using science-based approaches for recovering from complex PTSD.

The Healing Trauma Podcast - Focuses on using mindfulness, neuroscience and somatic modalities to release childhood developmental trauma being stored in the body and mind.

The Hilarious World of Depression - Candid interviews with celebrities and mental health experts offer insights on trauma with a dose of therapeutic humor.

Trauma Therapist podcast - Explains trauma types, interviews psychologists providing trauma therapy, and practical treatment insights. Some focus on complex PTSD and developmental trauma.

The Adult Chair Podcast - Host Michelle Chalfant weaves her lived experience, psychotherapy expertise and meditation practices into guidance for transforming complex trauma.

Beyond Surviving Podcast - Shares trauma treatment insights, survivor stories and book recommendations that promote hope, healing, empowerment and social change.

Therapy Chat Podcast - Interviews psychologists explaining current treatment approaches and research around PTSD, trauma, relationships, anxiety, self-esteem, and more.

YouTube Channels

The Crappy Childhood Fairy - Series by trauma-informed therapist Dan Fox on complex PTSD symptoms, coping skills, recovery concepts, and inner child work.

Patrick Teahan - Trauma-focused therapist discussing complex trauma, childhood wounds, healthy relationships, grief, internal family systems therapy.

Tim Fletcher - Complex Trauma Recovery - Psychologist specialized in developmental trauma recovery strategies through inner child work, grief, anger release.

Bessel van der Kolk - Many lectures by renowned trauma researcher on impacts of complex trauma, treatment approaches, implications for society.

Kelly Walker - Insightful videos on complex PTSD, dysfunctional families, inner child work, communication skills, assertiveness, codependency.

Therapy in a Nutshell - Emma McAdam LMFT shares trauma therapy insights though short animated videos. Uplifting.

The Crappy Childhood Fairy Recovery Helpers - Short clips demonstrating grounding, containment, emotional regulation, inner child and parts work techniques.

Trauma-Sensitive Mindfulness - Meditation teacher David Treleaven applies mindfulness and neuroscience specifically to support complex trauma recovery.

Online Support Forums

Psych Central PTSD Forums - Large online peer support community with forums on PTSD diagnosis, treatments, coping methods, med support, and managing life impacted by PTSD.

Trauma Survivors Network - Welcoming anonymized online community to share complex trauma experiences and seek peer support through forums and chat rooms.

After Narcissistic Abuse - Active support forums for survivors of narcissistic, sociopathic, psychopathic, abusive, or toxic relationships seeking validation and healing advice.

Mental Health Forum - Wide ranging forums on numerous mental health conditions including PTSD and complex trauma. Moderated, supportive peer exchange.

MyPTSD.com - Forums to share stories and seek advice divided between complex PTSD, dissociative disorders, less chronic forms of PTSD, and loved ones impacted by PTSD.

SAS - Selfhelp Support Forums - Large range of forums on mental health, personality disorders, PTSD, various forms of abuse, sexuality, identity issues. Peer moderated.

Documentaries

Resilience: The Biology of Stress and the Science of Hope (2017) - Details the impacts of adverse childhood experiences (ACEs) and toxic stress on health and behavior. Also explores promising interventions.

Promising Young Woman (2020) - Psychological drama film illustrating complex impacts and nonlinear recovery following sexual violence and betrayal trauma.

Childhood 2.0 (2020) - Experts and childhood trauma survivors discuss how adversity embeds in the brain and nervous system to affect development. Hopeful.

Paper Tigers (2015) - Inspirational chronicle of a rural high school's trauma-informed interventions with struggling teens that dramatically improved outcomes.

Heal (2017) - Explores the biological processes, traditional therapies and emerging treatments to cure systemic imbalances underlying trauma, addiction, mood disorders, autoimmunity.

Resilience (2016) - James Redford documentary profiles the adverse childhood experiences study (ACEs) and toxic stress impacts, as well as research on how people can heal.

Trauma: Who Will Listen? (2019) - Highlights barriers minorities face in seeking mental health support for trauma and features clinicians of color guiding recovery.

The Wisdom of Trauma (2021) - Interviews trauma experts on science of PTSD and collective trauma. Offers insights on using adversity for transformation.

This list provides a starting point of resources that can educate, support and guide your complex trauma recovery journey. Trust your intuition in finding additional assistance tailored to your unique needs and process. A multiplicity of paths lead to healing. You've got this. Keep going. Brighter days await.

References

American Psychiatric Association. (2013). Diagnostic and statistical manual of mental disorders (5th ed.). https://doi.org/10.1176/appi.books.9780890425596

Anda, R. F., Felitti, V. J., Bremner, J. D., Walker, J. D., Whitfield, C., Perry, B. D., Dube, S. R., & Giles, W. H. (2006). The enduring effects of abuse and related adverse experiences in childhood. European Archives of Psychiatry and Clinical Neuroscience, 256(3), 174-186. https://doi.org/10.1007/s00406-005-0624-4

van der Kolk, B. (2014). The body keeps the score: Brain, mind, and body in the healing of trauma. Penguin Books.

Schwartz, A. (2019). The complex PTSD workbook: A mind-body approach to regaining emotional control and becoming whole. Althea Press.

Walker, P. (2013). Complex PTSD: From surviving to thriving. CreateSpace Independent Publishing Platform.

Levine, P. A. (2010). In an unspoken voice: How the body releases trauma and restores goodness. North Atlantic Books.

Ogden, P., Minton, K., & Pain, C. (2006). Trauma and the body: A sensorimotor approach to psychotherapy. W.W. Norton & Co.

Fisher, J. (2017). Healing the fragmented selves of trauma survivors: Overcoming internal self-alienation. Routledge.

Najavits, L. M. (2002). Seeking safety: A treatment manual for PTSD and substance abuse. Guilford Press.

Herman, J. L. (2015). Trauma and recovery: The aftermath of violence--from domestic abuse to political terror. Basic Books.

Levine, P. A., & Frederick, A. (1997). Waking the tiger: Healing trauma : the innate capacity to transform overwhelming experiences. North Atlantic Books.

Rothschild, B. (2000). The body remembers: The psychophysiology of trauma and trauma treatment. W.W. Norton & Co.

Scaer, R. (2005). The trauma spectrum: Hidden wounds and human resiliency. W.W. Norton & Co.

Ringel, S. (2012). Trauma: Contemporary directions in theory, practice, and research. SAGE Publications.

Courtois, C. A. (2008). Complex trauma, complex reactions: Assessment and treatment. Psychological Trauma: Theory, Research, Practice, and Policy, S(1), 86-100. https://doi.org/10.1037/1942-9681.S.1.86

D'Andrea, W., Ford, J., Stolbach, B., Spinazzola, J., & van der Kolk, B. A. (2012). Understanding interpersonal trauma in children: Why we need a developmentally appropriate trauma diagnosis. American Journal of Orthopsychiatry, 82(2), 187-200. https://doi.org/10.1111/j.1939-0025.2012.01154.x

Herman, J. L. (1992). Complex PTSD: A syndrome in survivors of prolonged and repeated trauma. Journal of Traumatic Stress, 5(3), 377-391. https://doi.org/10.1007/BF00977235

Kinniburgh, K. J., Blaustein, M., Spinazzola, J., & van der Kolk, B. A. (2017). Attachment, self-regulation, and competency: A comprehensive intervention framework for children with complex trauma. Psychiatric Annals, 35(5), 424-430. https://doi.org/10.3928/00485713-20050501-08

Cook, A., Spinazzola, J., Ford, J., Lanktree, C., Blaustein, M., Cloitre, M., DeRosa, R., Hubbard, R., Kagan, R., Liautaud, J., Mallah, K., Olafson, E., & van der Kolk, B. (2017). Complex trauma in children and adolescents. Psychiatric Annals, 35(5), 390-398. https://doi.org/10.3928/00485713-20050501-05

Logan-Greene, P., Green, S., Nurius, P. S., & Longhi, D. (2014). Distress and coping among adult survivors of childhood sexual abuse as they undergo child forensic interviews. Journal of Child Sexual Abuse, 23(3), 264–286. https://doi.org/10.1080/10538712.2014.888118

Substance Abuse and Mental Health Services Administration. (2014). Trauma-informed care. Treatment Improvement Protocol Series 57. HHS Publication No. (SMA) 13-4801.

Cook, J. M., Dinnen, S., Rehman, O., Bufka, L., & Courtois, C. (2011). Responses of a sample of practicing psychologists to questions about clinical work with trauma and interest in specialized training. Psychological Trauma: Theory, Research, Practice, and Policy, 3(3), 253-257. http://dx.doi.org/10.1037/a0025048

Gentry, J.E. (2002). Compassion fatigue: A crucible of transformation. Journal of Trauma Practice, 1(3-4), 37-61. https://doi.org/10.1300/J189v01n03_03

Pearlman, L. A., & Courtois, C. A. (2005). Clinical Applications of the Attachment Framework: Relational

Treatment of Complex Trauma. Journal of Traumatic Stress, 18, 449-459. https://doi.org/10.1002/jts.20052

Fonagy, P., Luyten, P., & Allison, E. (2015). Epistemic petrification and the restoration of epistemic trust: A new conceptualization of borderline personality disorder and its psychosocial treatment. Journal of Personality Disorders, 29(5), 575-609. https://doi.org/10.1521/pedi.2015.29.5.575

De Bellis, M. D., Hooper, S. R., Woolley, D. P., & Shenk, C. E. (2010). Demographic, maltreatment, and neurobiological correlates of PTSD symptoms in children and adolescents. Journal of Pediatric Psychology, 35(5), 570–577. https://doi.org/10.1093/jpepsy/jsp116

Teicher, M. H., Samson, J. A., Anderson, C. M., & Ohashi, K. (2016). The effects of childhood maltreatment on brain structure, function and connectivity. Nature Reviews Neuroscience, 17(10), 652–666. https://doi.org/10.1038/nrn.2016.111

Thompson, B. L., & Waltz, J. (2010). Mindfulness and experiential avoidance as predictors of posttraumatic stress disorder avoidance symptom severity. Journal of Anxiety Disorders, 24(4), 409–415. https://doi.org/10.1016/j.janxdis.2010.02.005

Vujanovic, A. A., Niles, B., Pietrefesa, A., Schmertz, S. K., & Potter, C. M. (2013). Mindfulness in the treatment of posttraumatic stress disorder among military veterans. Spirituality in Clinical Practice, 1(S), 15-25. https://doi.org/10.1037/2326.4500.1.S.15

About the Author

Dr. Monday Farouq brings a profound sense of compassion and commitment to guiding others through the intricate process of recovering from complex PTSD. With over 15 years of experience as a clinical psychologist and trauma specialist, he is deeply familiar with both the challenges and the promise of this healing journey.

Dr. Farouq's motivation for writing this book stems from his own life mission to alleviate suffering and empower survivors. Early in his career, he was moved by the stories and struggles of many patients with complex developmental trauma. He soon developed a vision for integrating insights across psychotherapy, neuroscience, medicine, and his own cultural wisdom to offer a holistic approach tailored to the diverse needs of trauma survivors.

Over the years, Dr. Farouq has continued studying emerging science about the neurobiology of trauma and resilience while also volunteering in underserved communities.

All this knowledge and experience pour into his life's work - serving as a trusted guide for those ready to reclaim their peace and purpose. Through his thoughtful counseling, Dr. Farouq has assisted countless individuals to overcome symptoms, process difficult memories, build fulfilling relationships, and ultimately rewrite their stories from struggle to strength.

While complex PTSD presents profound challenges, Dr. Farouq balances scientific expertise with heartfelt optimism about the possibility of growth after adversity. He has witnessed firsthand how compassionate support and personal perseverance can transform suffering into wisdom. It is this spirit of hope that animates his writing and lights the way for those on the journey from hurt to wholeness.

Beyond his counseling practice, Dr. Farouq continues to advocate tirelessly for trauma-informed approaches and improved access to care. He also spends time mentoring the next generation of healers. Though his impact spans far beyond these pages, he considers this book - distilling hard-won knowledge into an accessible guide - one of his most meaningful contributions yet. It remains a privilege to walk with others through darkness into light.